The DOCTOR WHO
PATTERN BOOK

Published by arrangement with the
British Broadcasting Corporation

W.H. ALLEN · LONDON
1984

Typeset by Phoenix Photosetting, Chatham
Printed and bound in Great Britain by
Anchor Brendon Ltd, Tiptree, Essex
for the Publishers W.H. Allen & Co. PLC
44 Hill Street, London W1X 8LB

ISBN 0 491 03403 2

For
Walter, Jack and Emily

CONTENTS

INTRODUCTION

The BBC Television series *Doctor Who* is now into its third decade, a splendid record which few other television programmes can match. Its success rests on its tremendous variety and its appeal across such a wide spectrum of tastes. It is very entertaining, full of adventures in which good finally triumphs over evil, but not before it has been hung over several cliffs, sometimes literally. And it is tremendously imaginative. One of the beauties of science fiction is that a character can have one eye and three green legs and be totally believable.

Science fiction has fascinated people for hundreds of years; it is part of man's perpetual reach into the future. Since before Leonardo da Vinci drew his helicopter, people have struggled with and enjoyed speculating about the mind-boggling possibilities of space. Part of this speculation has been a preoccupation with the idea of travelling in time.

Another perpetual human fascination for which the *Doctor Who* series caters, is man's obsession with immortality. Alchemists and astrologers, witch doctors and wizards, professors and priests, as well as many millions of ordinary people have theories, dreams and convictions about eternal life.

Because *Doctor Who* touches our interest in all these ways, because it entertains us, intrigues us and fascinates us, many of us want to identify with the programme. What better way could there be than to dress like a favourite character, or to wear, live with or play with clothes, objects and toys that are derived from *Doctor Who.*

The obvious place to begin knitting was with Tom Baker's scarf. It has become a symbol of his regeneration of the Doctor, and the phrase 'Doctor Who scarf' has passed into the language even among people who are not devotees of the programme. From there the idea grew to include knitted and sewn clothes inspired by the programme, so that young people can dress as the characters, whilst still looking fashionable enough to please themselves, and smart enough to please their grannies! There are jumpers, too, to suit all ages, on which the programme name is proclaimed either loud and clear, or more subtly if you prefer. There are puppets and quilts, toys and cushions which will look equally at home on the family settee, or as part of the Whovian clutter of an enthusiast's own room.

If you have never knitted before there are several projects in the book that are very easy to do, notably the scarf and the puppets, and included is a how-to section on basic knitting to help you get started. Then you can progress to more ambitious projects, perhaps with a bit of help from your friends.

Above all, the patterns here are to enjoy, both in the making and in the wearing and owning, and the results, whether clothes or toys, will greatly add to the pleasure taken by every Doctor Who fan in the continuing adventures of the Doctor and his companions.

HOW TO KNIT

Knitted fabric, if you look at it closely, is simply rows and rows of holes tied together with yarn. Once you know how to make one of these holes (stitches), you can knit, simply by making lots of them. This makes it sound very easy – and it is! Once you are proficient in simple stitches, then you can graduate to the more complicated fancy stuff, but it is still only a matter of linking together in patterns those same holes or stitches as before. The first decision to make, is to choose what to make and what to make it with.

WHAT TO MAKE

The simplest shape to knit is a rectangle, so begin with this. But it needn't be a boring dishcloth or blanket square for a blanket that never gets done. Many lovely garments, such as tabards, T-shirts and tops can be made from rectangles. Have a go first at the Doctor Who scarf on page 37, about the longest rectangle you will ever want to do. Then try very simple shaping and cut the corners off your rectangles by making the puppets on page 70. Then you will be really on the way, and will have the tremendous satisfaction of having made something good yourself.

WHAT YARN TO CHOOSE

All sorts of yarns are available: made of natural fibres like wool, mohair (goat wool), angora (rabbit wool), cotton and linen; or of man-made fibres; or of mixtures of both. They can be thick or thin, hairy or smooth, lumpy or fine, multicoloured or plain, and almost any combination of these.

Out of this bewildering array it is best for a beginner to choose a fairly thick smooth yarn in, of course, whatever colour you like. But do avoid fine, fluffy or lumpy yarns to start with, as they will give you additional problems which you can do without. If you are making the scarf, why not take the photograph along to your yarn shop to get the colours as near as you can? The scarf is in an ideal beginner's yarn – chunky – and do stick to the same thickness of yarn throughout or very peculiar things will happen! The time to experiment with unusual or more difficult yarns is when you progress to the puppets. Have fun with them, trying out all the textures you are dying to have a go with; the puppets are on such a small scale that difficulties are in proportion – and, if they do turn out a little odd, you do not have to wear them.

CHOOSING NEEDLES

There is also a wide variety of needles, both in size and type. Most beginners prefer a fairly long needle, so that the stitches are not squashed together. So avoid short needles to start with (unless you are very young, in which case a shorter needle may fit your hand-size best). You will see circular needles and sets

of four double pointed needles too. Save both of these to experiment with later when you have got the hang of the straightforward kind. To choose your needle size (that is, its diameter rather than its length) you can use one of plenty of sources of advice. Firstly, the recommended size of needle for the yarn is now usually printed somewhere on the paper band around the ball of yarn. Secondly, if you are using a pattern it will usually recommend a needle size, or, thirdly, the staff of your wool shop should be able to advise you about needle size. You will see on most patterns a section at the beginning about tension or gauge. Deciding upon the tension at which you knit is the way of choosing the needle size for yourself, and is very important when garments particularly are knitted, and when doing your own design. But, since you cannot calculate tension until you can knit, it is written about at the end of this how-to section, so that you can use it in future projects.

BEGINNING TO KNIT

It can be very useful, when beginning to knit, to have someone with you who can already knit, to show you how. But, even without such help, you can teach yourself, step by step, following these instructions. If you are left-handed, you can choose to knit right-handed if you wish, or simply reverse all the instructions and drawings here, which are for the right-handed method. The easiest way to reverse the drawings, is to prop the book in front of a mirror and work from the mirror image. If someone is helping you to knit, then, if you are right-handed, ask them to sit alongside you with some knitting of their own and copy what they do. If you are left-handed, sit them opposite, facing you, and do with your right hand whatever they do with their left.

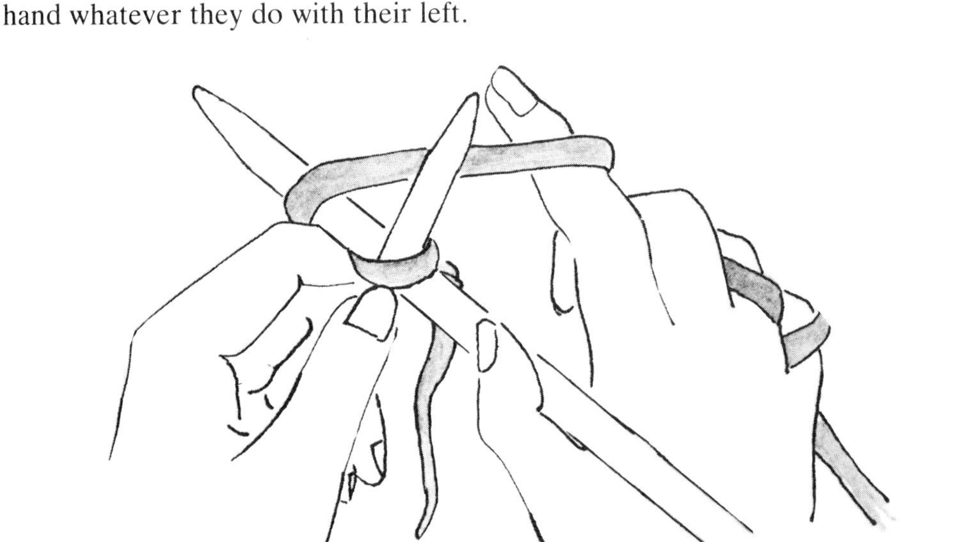

CASTING ON

This is the way you begin. If someone is helping you to learn, it is perhaps easier if, on your very first piece of work, they cast on for you and knit the first couple

of rows. This means that you can begin by learning to knit rather than learning to cast on first. However, if you are teaching yourself, begin here, and you will soon be knitting and you will also know how to cast on for yourself.

1. Make a slip loop in the beginning of the yarn and place it over the left-hand needle. Place the point of the right-hand needle through the front of the loop from front to back. Holding the yarn in your right hand, wind it round the point of the right-hand needle, only from back to front.

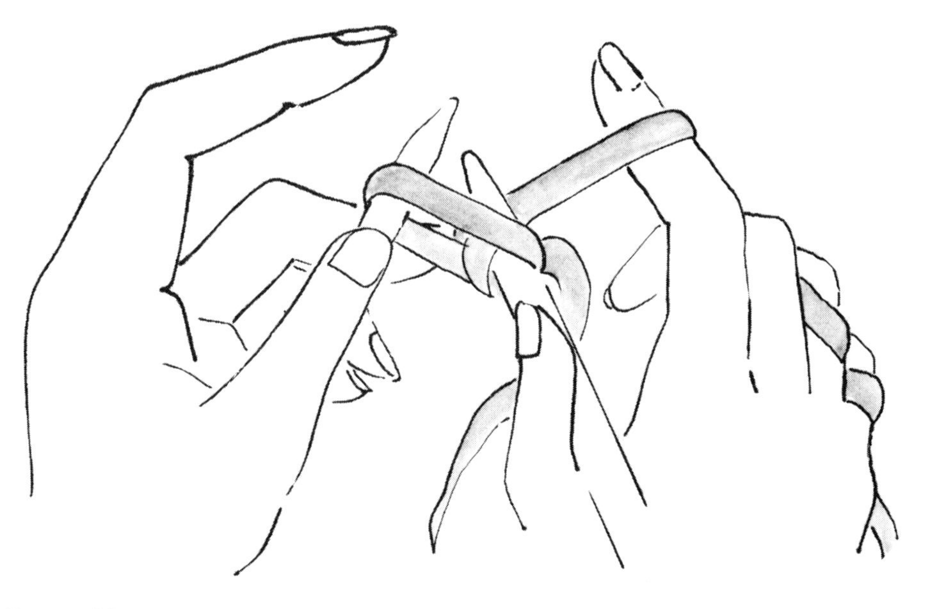

2. Draw this new loop which you have made towards you through the first slip loop.

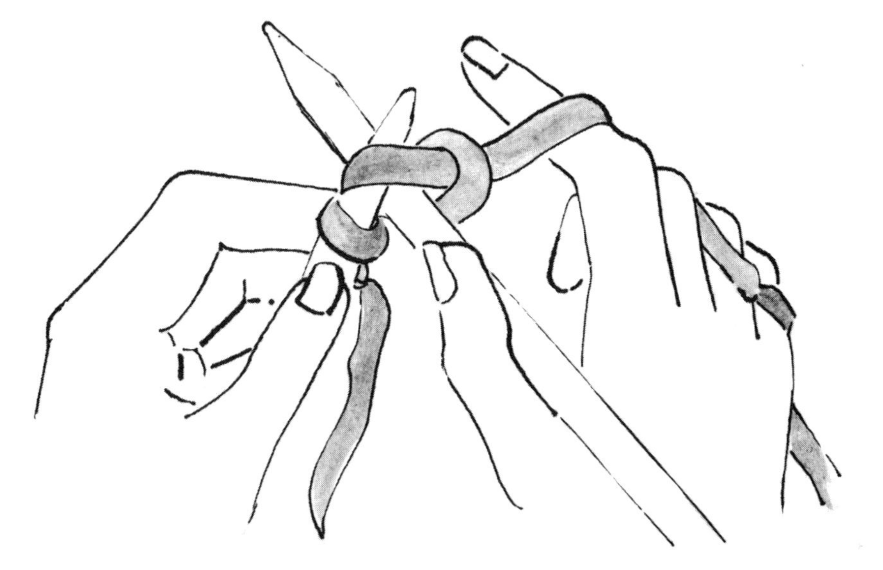

3. Pass this new loop from the right-hand needle onto the left-hand needle. Place the point of the right-hand needle from front to back through the front of this second new loop.

4. Now wind the yarn round the right-hand needle only, from back to front, then draw this third new loop which you have made, through the second loop, and pass this third loop from the right-hand needle onto the left-hand needle. Repeat this process until you have the correct number of loops, which are, of course, the stitches, on your left-hand needle.

There are several other ways of casting on which you can add to your repertoire of techniques later, but this is the easiest for a beginner. Do not allow casting-on to get too tight. Keep it loose, or it is very difficult to knit the first row.

TO KNIT

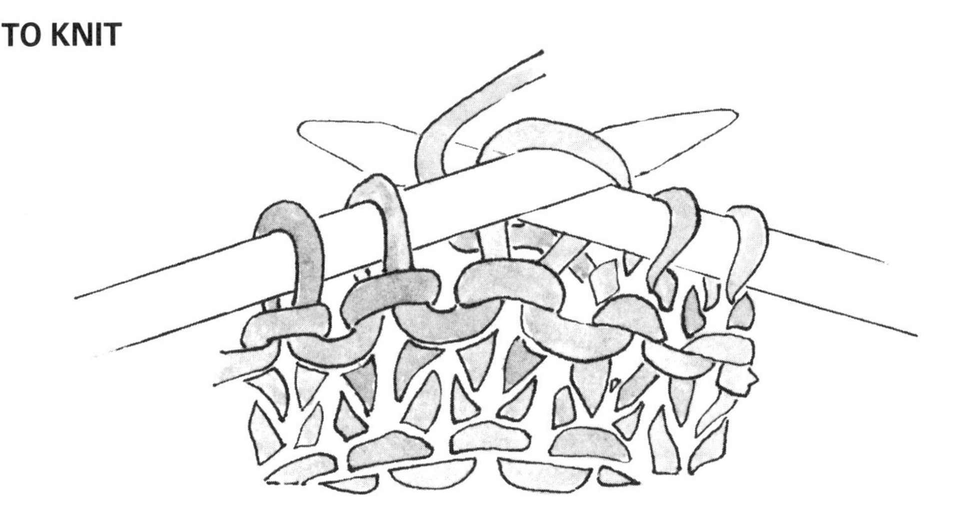

1. Hold the needle with the cast-on stitches on it in the left hand. Take the other needle in the right hand and insert its point through the front of the first stitch on the left-hand needle from front to back. Keeping the yarn at the back of the work, wind it under and over the point of the right-hand needle.

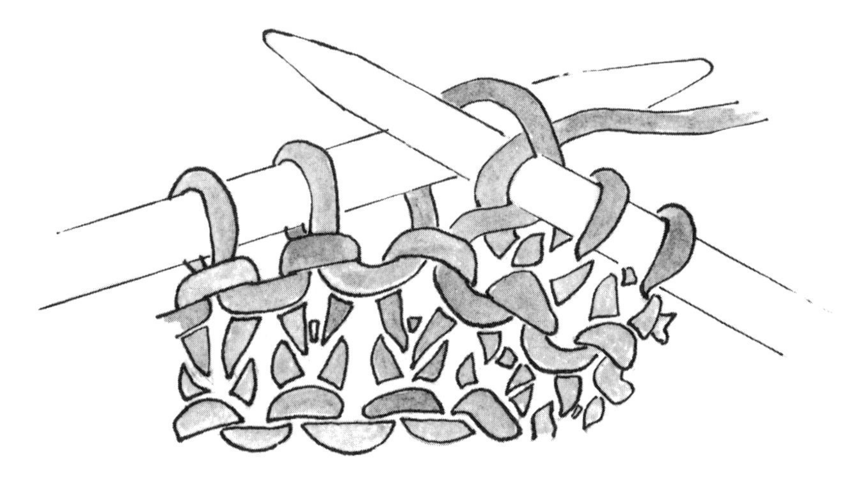

2. Then, using the point of the right-hand needle, draw the newly made loop through the stitch on the left-hand needle.

3. Keeping this newly made stitch on the right-hand needle, draw the old stitch, through which it passes, off the left hand needle, so completing your new stitch.

4. Repeat stages 1 to 3 with each stitch on the left-hand needle, transferring a new stitch onto the right-hand needle each time, until no stitches remain on the left-hand needle, and all have been transferred to the right, thus completing a row. To begin your next row, place the needle holding the stitches into your left hand, take the empty needle in your right hand and repeat the process.

Working in knit all the time like this produces garter stitch, or plain knitting, which is the stitch pattern used for the scarf. Be careful not to work too tightly, as this makes working very difficult, and mind you don't 'drop' stitches, that is, lose them from the needle, as they will ladder the work if you do. Ask an experienced knitter to pick up a stitch for you if you drop it. Work slowly to start with, and loosely, and you will soon find that you will speed up as your confidence grows.

TO CAST OFF

Casting off, also called binding off, is the way that work is finished off at the end. You cannot of course, simply remove the work from the needles. It would all unravel back to the beginning – most depressing!

In order to cast off, begin a new row in the usual way and knit two stitches. Then pick up the first of these two stitches on the point of the left-hand needle and pass it over the second stitch and off the right-hand needle, leaving the second stitch on its own on the right-hand needle.

Knit one more stitch, i.e. a third stitch, in the usual way, then pass the second stitch over the third in the same way as before, so leaving the third stitch alone on the right-hand needle. Repeat this until no stitches remain on the left-hand needle.

Break off the yarn. Pass it through the remaining stitch on the right-hand

needle and pull it tight. This completes the casting off. Do knit loosely on this casting off row as it can get very tight and distort the work if you are not careful.

TO PURL

The scarf was made in knit stitch, but, if you want to make more things, you need to know how to work in purl.

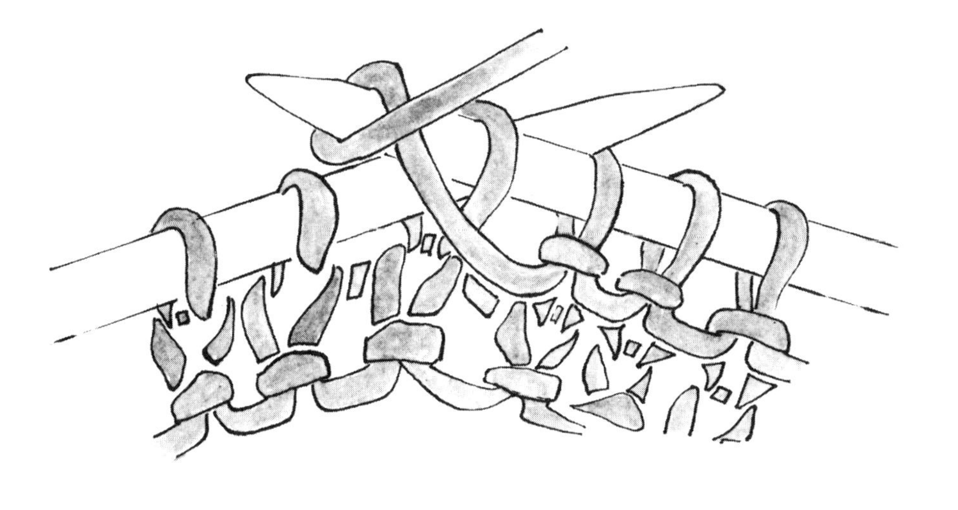

1. Cast on in the same way as before, then hold the needle with the cast-on stitches on it in the left hand. Take the other needle in the right hand and insert its point through the front of the first stitch (from right to left) on the left-hand needle. Keeping the yarn at the front of the work, pass it over and round the point of the right-hand needle.

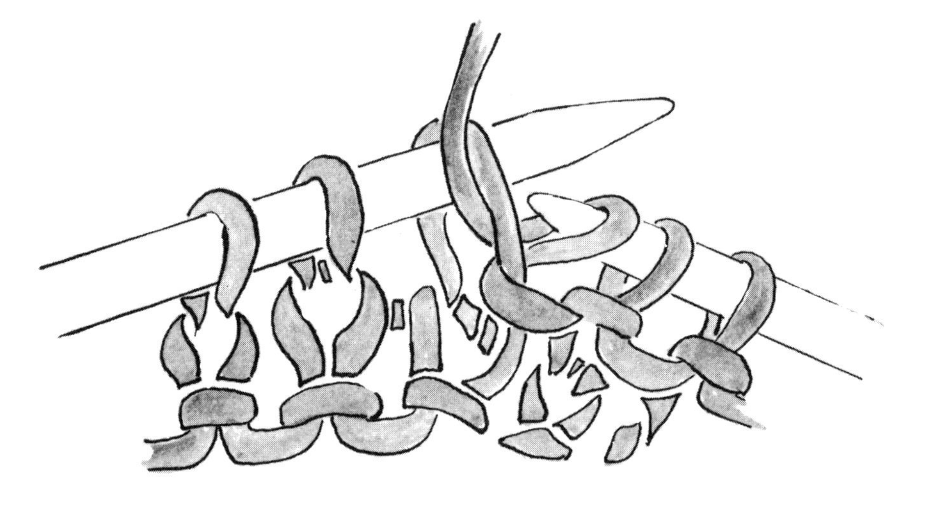

2. Using the point of the right-hand needle, draw the newly made loop through the stitch on the left-hand needle.

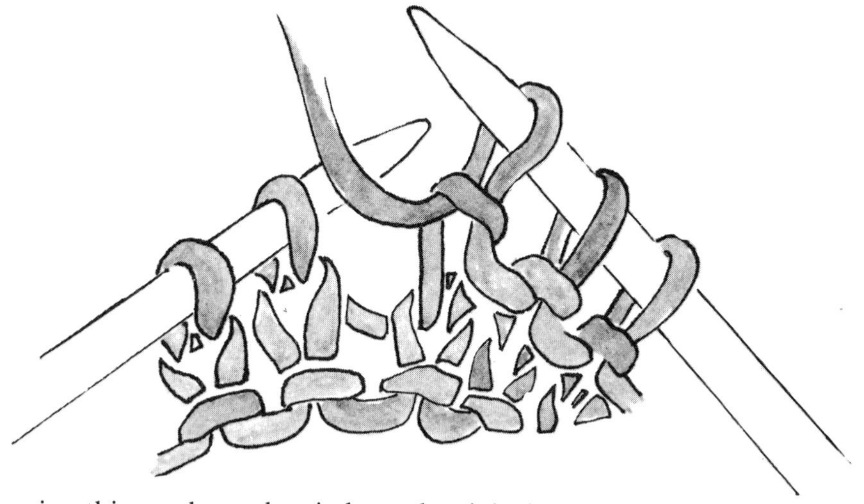

3. Keeping this newly made stitch on the right-hand needle, draw the old stitch, through which it passes, off the left-hand needle, so completing your new stitch.

Repeat this with each stitch on the left-hand needle, transferring a new purl stitch onto the right-hand needle each time, until no stitches remain on the left-hand needle, so completing a purl row.

STOCKING STITCH

Stocking stitch, also called stockinette stitch, is the familiar stitch from which so many jumpers – and for that matter, if you look closely, stockings – are made. It has the lovely smooth finish that so many traditional designs are based on. Many patterns call for it, and it is abbreviated as st.st.

To make stocking stitch, simply knit the first row, purl the second row, knit the third row, purl the fourth row, and so on, so working alternate rows of knit and purl throughout.

The fabric that results has a smooth side, called stocking stitch, and a rough side, which is sometimes used as a fabric in its own right, called reverse stocking stitch. Reverse stocking stitch is preferred in some patterns where a rough texture is required.

RIB OR RIBBING

The very elastic rib or welt used especially as the bottom edge, sleeve ends and neck bands of jumpers is made by alternating knit and purl stitches. Because these two kinds of stitch face different ways, this gives the fabric a wavy horizontal section and so make it stretchy.

Ribs are referred to in patterns as, for example: K1P1 rib. This means that, after casting on in the usual way, on your first row, you knit the first stitch with the yarn behind the work as usual for knitting, then pass the yarn through between the needle points to the front of the work, and purl the second stitch. Pass the yarn back to the wrong side and knit the third stitch, then return the yarn to the right side and purl the fourth stitch, and so on, working knit and purl stitches alternately, and therefore working a K1P1 rib row. On the second row, knit all the stitches that were purled on the previous row, and purl all the stitches

that were knitted on the previous row. The third row is like the first, and the fourth like the second, and so on until sufficient ribbed rows have been worked. Ribs can have as many stitches of each kind as you wish, for example, K2P2, or even K4P4, simply knit and purl the required number of stitches alternately on the first row, then continue working in the same way as for K1P1 rib.

Rib is often, on a garment, worked on needles which are smaller than those used for the main part of the garment, usually two sizes smaller. This gives the rib even greater elasticity.

DECREASING

If you go on to make the puppets, you will need to know how to decrease, which simply means to get rid of stitches and so reduce the width of the work. The usual way to do this is to knit two stitches together, (the abbreviation for this is written: K2tog). It can be done at either end, or in the middle, of a row.

Simply insert the point of the right-hand needle through the fronts of the next (or first) two stitches together, instead of through just one, and knit them both together, in the usual way, so converting two stitches into one.

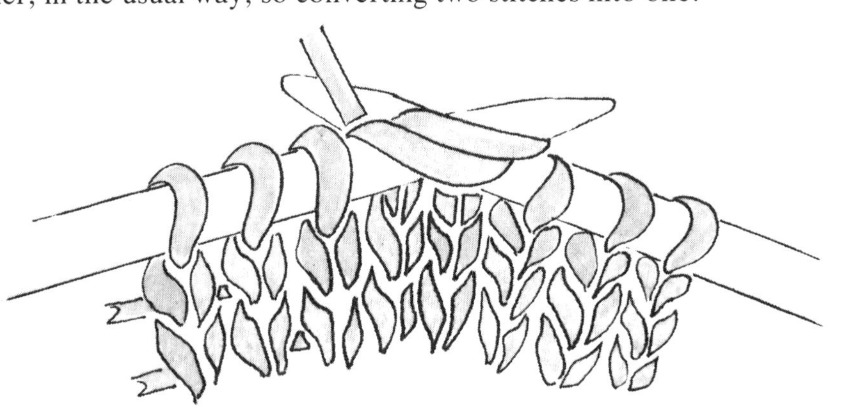

This creates a double stitch sloping to the right. Some patterns call for a stitch which slopes to the left, and this will be called: K2togtbl. This means knitting two stitches together through the back of the loops. To do this, insert the point of the right-hand needle through the backs of the next two stitches instead of through the fronts, then knit them both together in the usual way.

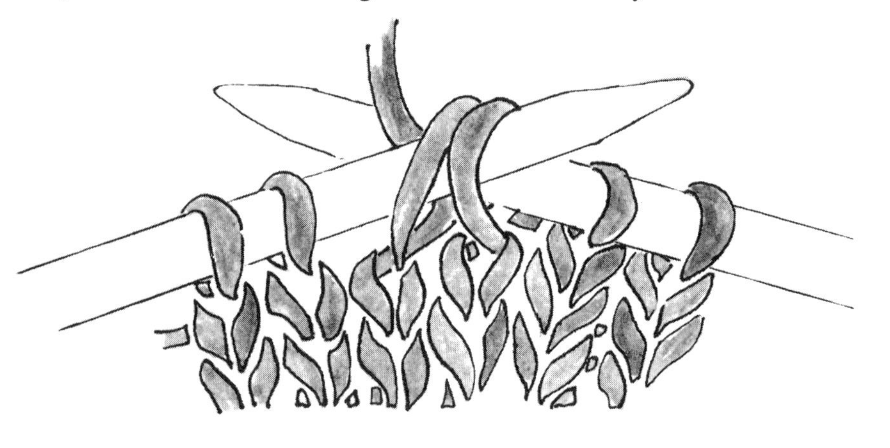

INCREASING

Sometimes, instead of wanting fewer stitches, and so decreasing, you may want to make more. If you wish to increase, for example by one stitch, at the beginning or end of a row, which is what is usually required in a pattern, this is what you do: knit or purl (whichever stitch you happen to be doing in the rest of the row) the first or last stitch in the ordinary way. Do not, however, as usual, slip the stitch off the point of the left-hand needle. Instead, re-insert the point of the right-hand needle into the back thread of the same stitch. Knit or purl this thread also, only then allowing the old stitch to come off the left-hand needle, so making two stitches on the right-hand needle out of just one stitch from the previous row.

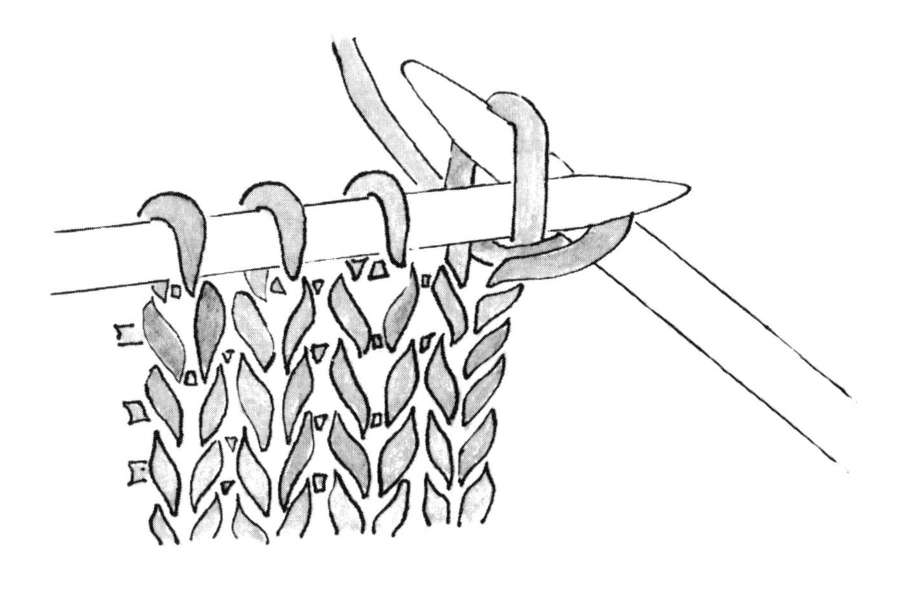

This method of increasing, also called making a stitch, or working two stitches in one stitch, can also be done in the middle of a row if required.

SWISS DARNING OR DUPLICATE STITCH

Several patterns in this book recommend this way of decorating a piece of knitting and it is certainly the easiest way for beginners to bring different colours into their work, but remember that it only works really satisfactorily on stocking stitch.

After the knitting is complete, decide what you would like to embroider on it, and where, perhaps using one of the charts given later in the book for a knitted pattern.

1. With a length of your contrasting yarn threaded through a blunt sewing or tapestry needle, fasten on firmly and as invisibly as possible on the wrong side. Bring your thread up on to the right side of the work though the bottom of a

knitted stitch, then pass your sewing needle under both strands of the knitted stitch of the row above, from right to left.

2. Pull the yarn flat but not tight. Then pass your sewing needle back down through the bottom of the stitch where your needle first came out, and then up again onto the right side at the bottom of the next stitch, so passing beneath two strands of yarn on the row below, from right to left.

3. Again pull the yarn flat but not tight, so creating, in embroidery, a duplicate of the knitted stitch beneath, but in a different colour, hence the name duplicate stitch. Repeat as often as necessary in whatever colours you wish, to create the design you want.

TENSION OR GAUGE

In almost all knitting patterns, including the ones in this book, you will see a reference to tension or gauge. This simply means the number of stitches and rows per inch which a particular piece of knitting achieves, This is, of course governed by the size of each stitch.

If you do more knitting, and perhaps begin to design for yourself, you need to know how to measure tension because the size of the garment you are making – suppose it is meant to be 34 inches all round – will be dictated by the number of stitches and their size.

For example, if there are 6 stitches per inch, there will be 204 stitches all around your garment. But imagine what will happen if each of your stitches is a little bigger so that there are only 5 stitches per inch. If you still have 204 stitches, the distance round the garment will be 204 divided by 5, which is over 40 inches i.e. three sizes too big!

To get your tension correct, use the recommended needles and cast on enough stitches to give a width of about 5 inches at the recommended tension. Work in the stitch pattern suggested until you have a 5-inch square, and cast off loosely (or, if you are brave enough, simply slip the work off the needle and handle it carefully). Measure – across the central 4 inches how many stitches per inch you have. Compare this with the recommended tension. Too many stitches per inch? Your stitches are too small. Change to needles one size larger and knit another square. Too few stitches per inch? Your stitches are too large. Change to needles one size smaller and knit another square. Continue doing this until your tension is the same as the recommended one, then knit your garment on needles which are the size you have chosen (because they suit the way you knit).

If other needle sizes are given in the pattern, for example, welts and ribbing are usually worked on needles two sizes smaller than those used for the main part, then you too should used needles two sizes smaller than the ones you have chosen to achieve the recommended tension.

MAKING UP

When you have knitted a garment, you will of course, unless you have been very clever, have several pieces of work which need fastening together. If you began with the scarf, then this does not apply, but you could practise sewing together the two halves of a puppet. Here are a few points which might help. Very few yarns today need pressing, and it is better only to consider pressing wool yarns. If you do press, pin the garment piece out first, then press with a warm iron gently on a damp cloth.

When pinning knitting together, use the easily visible large coloured-headed pins, as dressmakers pins get lost in the yarn with potentially nasty consequences! Pin both ends first, then middle to middle, then the middles of each half, and so on. This matches the knitting evenly; otherwise, knitting is so stretchy that if you begin at one end and work towards the other, almost

certainly, one piece will turn out longer than the other. Always check that you have matched any shapings or patterns that should be matched, before you begin to sew.

Use the yarn with which you knitted to sew the garment up, so that it does not show, and so that it behaves and washes like the rest of the garment. The only exceptions to this are the very hairy or lumpy yarns which are horrible to sew with. For these, choose as near a match as you can in a similar smooth yarn. Sew the pieces together with a stitch that will stretch, like back stitch, and fasten on and off well at the beginning and end of a seam.

GUIDE TO USING PATTERNS

All the patterns in this book are graded according to difficulty. You will find the following symbols indicating the varying levels of skill required to make the garments and objects alongside the heading for each item:

☆ Could be made by children and others with only basic skills, with a little help

☆☆ Average skill needed

☆☆☆ Extra skill needed

KNITTING CHARTS

Charts for the picture knitting are a stitch by stitch diagram of what colours to knit. The first and every alternate odd-numbered row will always be knitted and worked from right to left on the diagram, beginning your first contrasting coloured stitch as given in the particular pattern. The second and every alternate even-numbered row will always be purled, and worked from left to right on the diagram. As you go along, you will be able to relate the coloured stitches in the row which you are working, to those in the previous row, and so watch the picture grow.

SEWING PATTERNS

Detailed instructions for using the sewing patterns (pages 106–117) are given on page 105 and should be read carefully before you begin work on the item.

DOCTOR
WHO

DOCTOR
WHO

USEFUL INFORMATION

MATERIALS USED

Throughout this book I hope that you will use whatever fabrics and yarns you like, or are available to you. Certainly the fabrics I used were chosen simply for their colour and suitability, and in case you would like to use exactly the same yarns as I did, here is a list of them, with the exception of the knitted nasty glove puppets and the costumes for the six different Doctors, for which I used any suitable available and interesting scraps.

K9 Cushion:	Patons' Beehive Double Knitting
Romana's T-Shirt:	Wendy Choice 4 Ply
Yeti:	Jaeger Mohair Spun
Scarf:	Sirdar Country Style Chunky
Cricket Jumper:	Wendy Choice Double Knitting
Nyssa's Jacket:	Patons Moorland Shetland Double Knitting
Neon Jumper:	Wendy Ascot Double Knitting
Starburst Jumper:	Patons Beehive Double Knitting with Twilleys Silver Goldfingering thread
Diamond Jumper:	Sirdar Country Style Double Knitting

In the event of any of the yarns being difficult to obtain, the following addresses will prove helpful:
Wendy Wools: Carter & Parker Ltd, Guiseley, West Yorkshire LS20 9PD;
White Buffalo Mills Ltd, 545 Assinboine Avenue, Brandon, Manitoba 7272401, Canada;
White Buffalo Mills Ltd, P.O. Box 506, Lynbrook, New York 11563, USA

Patons: Patons and Jaeger Ltd, Patons and Baldwin Ltd, P.O. Box, Darlington DL1 1YQ

Sirdar: Sirdar PLC, Flanshaw Lane, Alverthorpe, Wakefield, West Yorkshire WF2 9ND;
Kendex Corporation, 31332 Via Colinas, 107 Westlake Village, California 91362, USA;
Diamond Yarn (Canada) Corp., 153 Bridgeland, Unit 11, Toronto M6A 2Y6, Ontario, Canada

Twilleys: H.G. Twilley Ltd, Roman Mill, Stamford, Lincolnshire PE9 1BG;
Panda Yarns, 17/27 Brunswick Road, East Brunswick, 3057 Victoria, Australia;
S.R. Kertzer & Co. Ltd, 257 Adelaide St West, Toronto, Ontario, Canada; also widely available in the USA.

AMERICAN AND BRITSH KNITTING TERMS

UK	US
brackets	parentheses
cast off	bind off
stocking stitch	stockinette stitch
swiss darning (*working a motif over knitted fabric*)	duplicate stitch
tension	gauge
work straight	work even
yarn over needle / yarn round needle	yarn over
yarn forward	bring yarn to front of work
yarn back	bring yarn to back of work

KNITTING NEEDLE SIZES

Original UK	000	00	0	1	2	3	4	5	6
Metric (mm)	9	8½	8	7½	7	6½	6	5½	5
USA	15	13	—	11	10½	10	9	8	7

Original UK	7	8	9	10	11	12	13	14
Metric (mm)	4½	4	3½ & 3¾	3¼	2¾ & 3	2½	2¼	2
USA	6	5	4	3	2	1	0	00

ABBREVIATIONS

alt. = alternate
approx. = approximately
beg. = beginning
cm = centimetre(s)
cont. = continue
dec. = decrease
foll. = following
gm = gram(s)
g.st. = garter stitch (i.e. every row K)
in = inch(es)
inc. = increase
K = knit
kg = kilogram(s)
m = metre(s)
mm = millimetre(s)
moss st. = moss stitch i.e.
1st row: K1P1, rep. to end.
2nd row: P1K1, rep. to end.
P = purl
psso = pass slip stitch over
rem. = remaining
rep. = repeat
rev.st.st. = reverse side of stocking stitch
sl. = slip
st(s). = stitch(es)
st.st. = stocking stitch
tbl = through back of loop i.e. through the back of the stitch
tog = together
togtbl = together through back of loop
yd = yard

BASIC DOUBLE KNITTING JUMPER ☆☆

Sizes
To fit chest/bust 26(28 30 32 34 36 38 40 42)in, 66(71 76 81 86 91 97 102 107)cm.

Materials
5(5 6 8 9 9 10 11 12) × 50gm balls of double knitting yarn in main colour.
1 pair of size 8 (4mm, US size 5) needles. 1 pair of size 10 (3¼mm, US size 3) needles.

Tension
24 sts. and 32 rows = 4in (10cm) in st.st. on size 8 (4mm, US size 5) needles

Front
Using size 10 (3¼mm, US size 3) needles, cast on 85(91 97 103 109 115 121 127 133) sts.

1st row: K1, *P1, K1, rep. from * to end.
2nd row: P1,*K1, P1, rep. from * to end.
Rep. these two rows until 2in (5cm) of rib has been worked.

Change to size 8 (4mm, US size 5) needles and st.st. Cont. in st.st. until work measures 10½(11½ 12½ 13 14½ 16 16½ 17 17½)in, 27(29 32 33 37 41 42 43 44) cm, or required length, ending with a P row.

To shape armholes:
Cast off 5(5 5 5 4 5 5 6 6) sts. at beg. of next two rows.
Next row: K3, K2togtbl, K to last 5 sts., K2tog, K3.
Next row: P.
Rep. these two rows until 39(41 45 47 47 47 49 49 53) sts. remain, ending with a P row.

To shape neck:
Next row: K3, K2togtbl, K18(19 22 24 24 24 26 26 28) sts., slip the last 7(7 9 11 11 11 13 13 13) sts. just worked onto a stitch holder, K to last 5 sts., K2tog, K3.
Next row: P.
Cont. to dec. at armhole edge as before, and cast off 2(2 3 3 3 3 3 3 2) sts. at the beg. (neck edge) of the next and foll. 3(3 2 2 2 2 2 2 4) alt.rows. Cont. to dec. at armhole edge only until 3 sts. remain, K3tog. Fasten off.
Rejoin yarn at neck edge to rem.sts. and work to match other side, reversing all shapings and working armhole shapings K2togtbl, not K2tog.

Back

Using size 10 (3¼mm, US size 3) needles, cast on 85(91 97 103 109 115 121 127 133) sts.

Work 2in (5cm) rib as given for front.

Change to size 8 (4mm, US size 5) needles and st.st. Cont. in st.st. until work measures 10½(11½ 12½ 13 14½ 16 16½ 17 17½)in, 27(29 32 33 37 41 42 43 44)cm, or required length to armhole, ending with a P row.

To shape armholes:
Cast off 5(5 5 5 4 5 5 6 6) sts. at beg. of next two rows.

Next row: K3, K2togtbl, K to last 5 sts., K2tog, K3.
Next row: P.
Rep. these two rows until 29(31 33 35 35 35 37 37 39) sts. remain, slip these sts. on to a stitch holder.

Sleeves

Make two, both alike.
Using size 10 (3¼mm, US size 3) needles, cast on 39(41 43 45 53 53 55 59 63) sts.

Work 2in (5cm) rib as given for front.
Change to size 8 (4mm, US size 5) needles and st.st. Cont. in st.st. and inc. 1 st. at each end of the 7th and every foll. 6th row until there are 55(55 57 57 59 59 61 85 89) sts., and then on every 8th row until there are 57(61 65 69 75 81 85 91 95) sts.
Then work straight until work measures a total of 12½(13½ 14½ 15½ 16½ 16½ 17½ 18 18½)in, 32(34 37 39 42 42 44 46 47)cm or required length, ending with a P row.

To shape top:
Cast off 5(5 5 5 4 5 5 6 6) sts. at beg. of next two rows.

Next row. K3, K2togtbl, K to last 5 sts., K2tog, K3.
Next row: P.
Next row: K.
Next row: P.
Rep. these last four rows 2(2 2 2 1 1 1 2 2) times more, then the first two rows only until 9 sts. remain.

For sizes 26 28 30 32 34 36 38in (66 71 76 81 86 91 97cm) only:
Next row: K3, sl. 1, K2tog, psso, K3.
Next row: P.

For all sizes:
Slip remaining sts. onto a safety-pin.

Making up and neckband

Join left and right front raglan seams, and left back raglan seam.

With right side of work facing, using size 10 (3¼mm, US size 3) needles, K29(31 33 35 35 35 37 37 39) sts. from back of neck, 7(7 7 7 7 7 7 9 9) sts. from sleeve top, pick up and K14(14 16 16 16 18 18 18 18) sts. down left side of neck, K7(7 9 11 11 11 13 13 13) sts. from front of neck, pick up and K13(13 15 15 15 17 17 17 17) sts. up right side of neck, K7(7 7 7 7 7 7 9 9) sts. from sleeve top. This gives a total of 77(79 87 91 91 95 99 99 105) sts.

Work 3in (8cm) rib as given for front.

Cast off loosely in rib.
Join all remaining seams.
Turn neckband onto wrong side and loosely slip stitch down.

DIAMOND JUMPER ☆☆

This flamboyant title logo from the *Doctor Who* series (see chart on p. 26) is often in the colours used here but you can, of course, use others if you wish. The lettering is often black or a plain primary colour, and the lettering only, without the diamond, also evokes the programme. If you plan to alter the chart in this way, remember to choose colours which contrast enough with the background to keep the lettering legible. The diamond shape is about 8in (20cm) high and 8in (20cm) across, and placed on this jumper at about underarm height. You can of course place it wherever you wish. Colour illustration is on page 20.

Materials

In addition to the main yarn (see Basic Double Knitting Jumper pattern on page 23) you will need small quantities of bright red, white and orange yarn.

To make

Make the Basic Jumper from page 23, but place the motif from the chart in the following way. Decide upon the length which you are going to work to the armhole, either that given in the pattern or your chosen length. Then work in plain st.st. until 4in (10cm) before you reach this length on the five larger sizes (34in – 42in or 86cm – 107cm) and 5in (13cm) before this length on the four smaller sizes (26in – 32in or 66cm – 81cm) ending with a P row. The following K

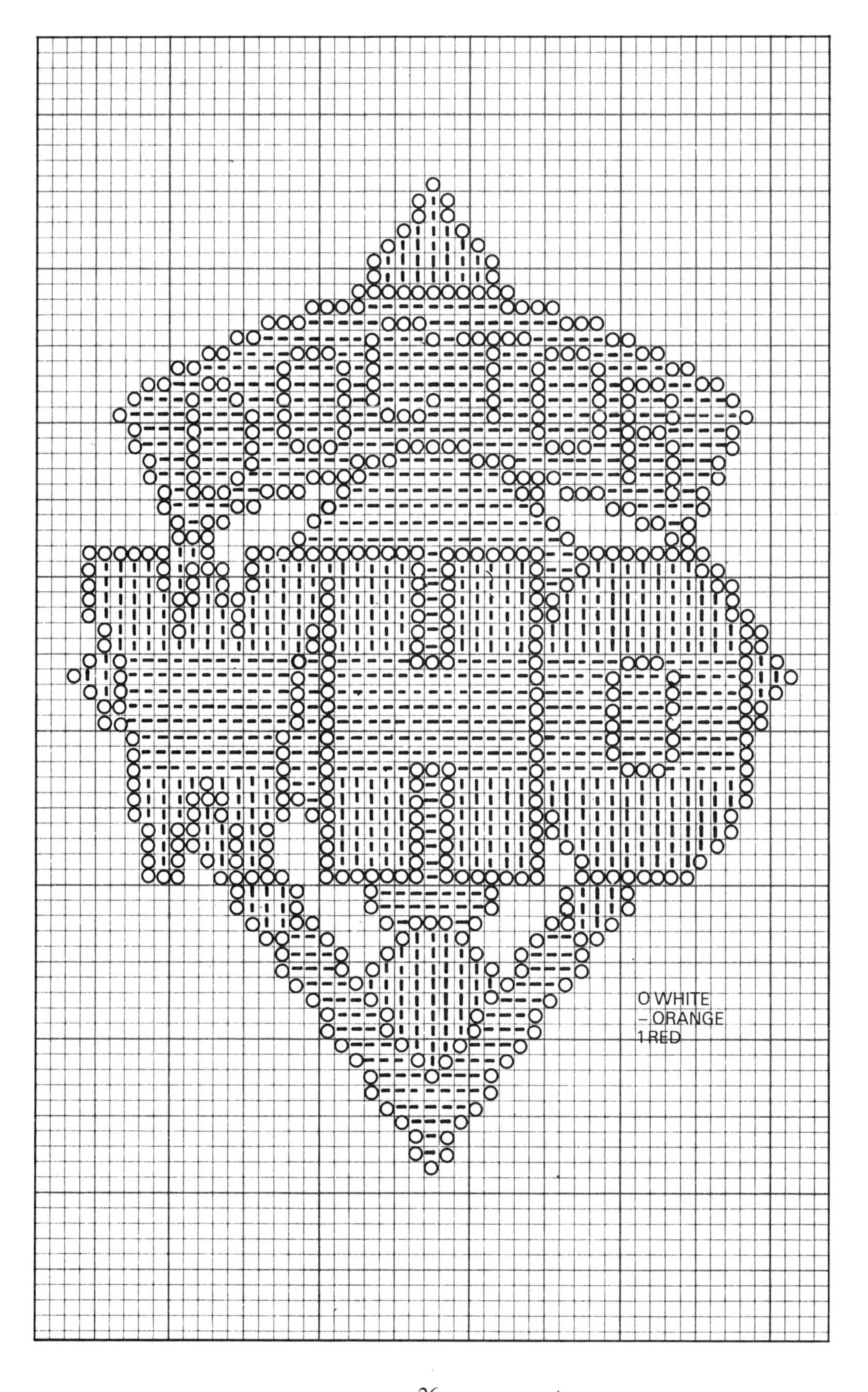
O WHITE
– ORANGE
1 RED

row is the first of the chart. The first and only black stitch on the first row of the pattern chart is stitch number 43(46 49 52 55 58 61 64 67) of your first chart row (i.e. the middle stitch for the size you are knitting).

NEON JUMPER☆☆

The current *Doctor Who* logo looks as if it is made of neon tubing, and is widely used on the books and comics. Put the series name in light on your jumper with a fairly discreet motif, about 6in (15cm) across and placed as a badge. If you prefer to shout your allegiance to the Doctor, then knit in a diamond pattern on page 25. This more subtle badge is Swiss darned, that is, worked in duplicate stitch, after the raglan sleeved jumper is complete. It is very easy, especially for a small pattern made up of lines as this one is. (See the how-to section, page 7, if you have never done this stitch before.) Colour illustration is on p. 19.

Materials

Additional material required to those shown in the basic jumper pattern is a small quantity of yellow double knitting yarn for the motif.

To make

The motif is placed with the top outside corner of the D in the word 'Doctor' 2in (5cm) from the right front raglan seam, and 4in (10cm) down from the shoulder. You can of course, place it where you wish. It measures approximately 6in × 2½in (15cm × 6cm). Swiss darn, or duplicate stitch, the motif from the chart in yellow.

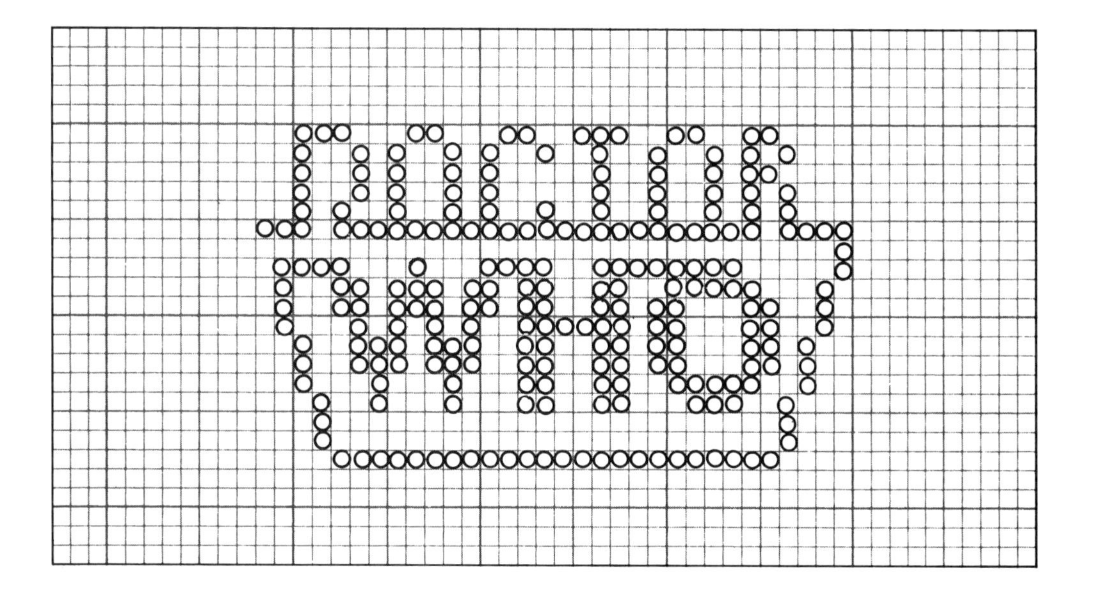

STARBURST JUMPER☆★

The famous and exciting *Doctor Who* music, when the series was younger, played against a whirling vortex, an almost impossible pattern to reproduce in knitting, and a distinctly peculiar shape to wear. More recently however, we have been greeted by swirling points of light gathering themselves into a constellation which gradually resolves itself into the Doctor's face. This process, caught at the stage where the face is discernable, but still made of stars, makes a most exciting picture to knit. The 'stars' are knitted here in white double knitting yarn and a fine silver yarn used together, but you could use white double knitting yarn on its own, or any metallic, preferably silver, yarn that knits to the same tension as the main yarn used for the jumper.

The chart (page 33) is for the central picture of the face, the remaining scattered stars are embroidered in Swiss darning or duplicate stitch at random and to your own taste. If you can, try to weave in the strands of white and silver yarn that cross the back of the work as much as possible without them showing on the right side, otherwise the loops on the reverse will catch in wear.

If you prefer, the whole picture can be Swiss darned, instead of knitted in, and you can, of course, use any colours you like.

Materials

Amounts as given for the basic jumper of dark navy blue double knitting yarn. Also 1 × 50gm ball of white double knitting; one large reel of thin silver thread.

Measurements

As given in the Basic Jumper pattern (page 23).

To make

Follow the Basic Jumper pattern, working the picture from the chart into the front as follows:

Begin with the silver/white stitch marked × on the chart, making this stitch number 23(26 29 32 35 38 41 44 47) of row 15(19 23 27 35 43 47 51 55) of st.st., beginning the st.st. after the rib with a K row, to ensure that the first row of the chart is also K. All marked stitches on the chart are in white/silver, all remaining stitches are in the background colour.

When the front is completed, work the remaining 'stars' as single stitches of Swiss darning, or duplicate stitch, in the star colour, taking care not to pull the yarn too tightly behind the work, and darning loops in as much as possible without letting them show through on the right side. The stars are arranged totally at random around the face. Scatter them widely, because if they are too closely packed around the face, it will loose its definition, and arrange them in groups rather than in lines so that they look like a night sky scattered with constellations.

PUBLIC CALL
BOX

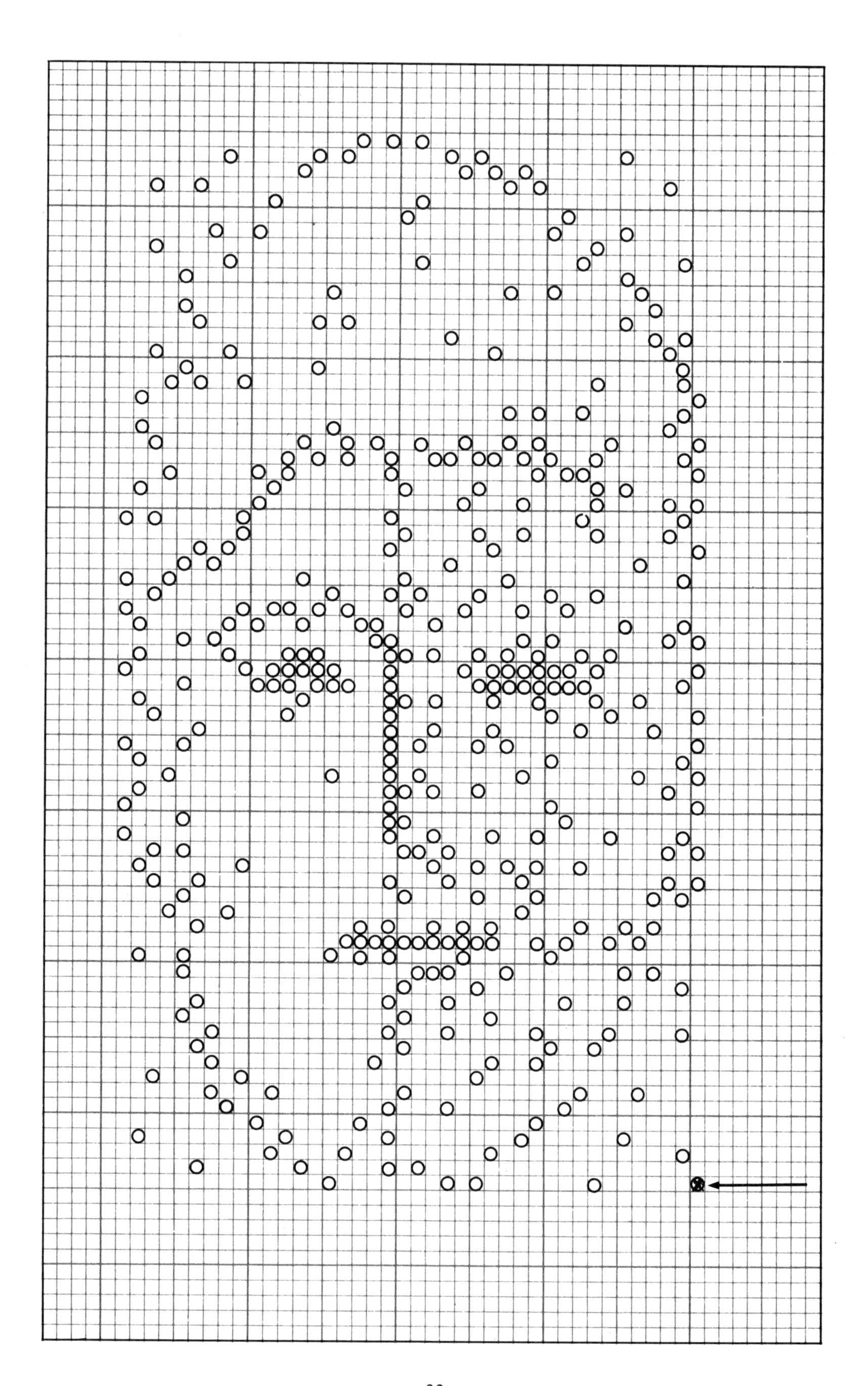

CRICKET JUMPER☆☆

Peter Davison's fifth incarnation of the Doctor considers himself rather sporting and so the cricketing gear is most appropriate. The jumper, in double knitting yarn, can be used for real cricket too, of course, as well as for play-acting, and is a sporting, comfortable fit.

If you want to wear a more complete Doctor costume, line the collar and face the opening of a white shirt with red ribbon or material, and embroider question marks in red on the collar points. If you have a cream blazer or jacket, and if no one minds, bind the edges with a red braid. Ideally, this should be a long frock coat, but not many people wear these nowadays of course. To finish off the outfit make the stick of celery brooch (see page 84 and pattern on page 111, and pin it on your lapel. Finally, decorate a white Panama-style hat with faintly spotted red ribbon. Colour illustration is on page 32.

Sizes

To fit chest/bust 32(34 36 38 40)in, 81(86 91 97 102)cm.

Materials

8(8 8 9 9)× 50gm balls of white double knitting yarn, and small quantities of black, bright red and brown yarn.

Tension

24 sts. and 32 rows = 4in (10cm) in st.st. on size 8 (4mm, US size 5) needles. Over pattern the tension is 28 sts. and 32 rows = 4in (10cm) on size 8 (4mm, US size 5) needles.

Back

Using size 10 (3¼mm, US size 3) needles cast on 107(113 119 125 133) sts.

1st row: K1,*P1, K1, rep. from * to end.
2nd row: P1,*K1, P1, rep. from * to end.
Rep. the last 2 rows until 2½in (6cm) of rib have been worked.
Next row: Rib 5(8 3 6 10), *inc. 1 st. in next st., rib 7*, rep. from * to * to last 6(9 4 7 11) sts., inc. 1 st. in next st., rib to end. (120 126 134 140 148 sts.)

Change to size 8 (4mm, US size 5) needles and pattern as follows:
1st row: K1(4 8 2 6), P2, K6, *P2, K8, P2, K6 *, rep. from * to * to last 3(6 10 4 8) sts., P2, K to end.
2nd row: P1(4 8 2 6), K2, P6, *K2, P8, K2, P6 *, rep. from * to * to last 3(6 10 4 8) sts., K2, P to end.
These 2 rows form the basic rib, cont. in the same way for 4 more rows.

7th row: work cabling as follows:
K1(4 8 2 6), P2, cable 6, *P2, K8, P2, cable 6 in same direction *, rep. from * to * to last 3(6 10 4 8) sts., P2, K to end.
Keeping basic rib correct, cont. in this way, cabling as for cable row on every 14th row from now on throughout the work.
Work to a total of 15½in (39cm) or required length to underarm, finishing at the end of a wrong side row. **

To shape armholes keep pattern correct throughout remainder of work and shape as follows:
Cast off 5 sts. at beg. of next 2 rows.
Dec. 1 st. at each end of next and every foll. alt. row to 94(100 108 114 122) sts. i.e. work 8 dec. rows, 16 rows altogether.
Work until armhole measures 8½in (22cm).

To shape shoulder:
Cast off 9(10 11 12 13) sts. at beg. of next 6 rows. Leave rem. 40(40 42 42 44) sts. on a holder.

Front

Work exactly as for back as far as **i.e. before beginning to shape armholes.

To shape armholes and neck, keep pattern correct throughout remainder of work and shape as follows:
Cast off 5 sts. at beg of next row, work 54(57 61 64 68) sts., turn and leave rem. 61(64 68 71 75) sts. on a holder.
Cont. on the 54(57 61 64 68) sts. shaping armhole as before, i.e. losing 1 st. at this armhole edge on next 8 alt. rows, *at the same time* dec. 1 st. at neck edge on every alt. row 19(19 20 20 21) times, giving 27(30 33 36 39) sts.
Work until armhole matches that on the back i.e. until armhole measures 8½in (22cm), finishing at armhole edge.
Cast off 9(10 11 12 13) sts. at beg. of next and next alt. row.
Work 1 row.
Cast off rem. 9(10 11 12 13) sts.

Rejoin yarn to centre front of work.
K2togtbl and leave this st. on a safety-pin, work in pattern to end of row 59(62 66 69 73) sts.
Work this side to match the first, shaping armhole and neck edge as for first side.

Sleeves

In white, both alike.
Cast on 52(54 56 56 58) sts. on size 10 (3¼mm, US size 3) needles and work in K1 P1 rib as given for the back for 2½in (6cm).

Change to size 8 (4mm, US size 5) needles and work as follows:
1st row: K21(22 23 23 24) sts., P2, K6, P2, K21(22 23 23 24) sts.
2nd row: P21(22 23 23 24) sts., K2 P6, K2, P21(22 23 23 24) sts.
Continue in this way, working a single cable throughout the sleeve and cabling on the 7th and every foll. 14th row, *at the same time* inc. 1 st. each end of the 3rd and every foll. 4th row to 84 sts.

Keeping single cable correct work until sleeve measures a total of 17in (43cm) or required underarm length ending with a wrong side row.

To shape top of sleeve:
Cast off 5 sts. at beg. of next 2 rows.
Dec. 1 st. at each end of next and every foll. alt. row to 40 sts.
Cast off 2 sts. at beg of every row to 12 sts.
Cast off.

Neckband

Join left shoulder seam.
With right side of work facing, using smaller needles and white yarn, pick up and K onto wrong side 40(40 42 42 44) sts. left at back neck, 56(56 58 58 58) sts. evenly down left side of neck (approx. 6 sts. per inch or per 2½cm), 1 st. from pin at centre front, (leave this stitch marked by the pin) and 56(56 58 58 58) sts. evenly up right side of neck. This gives 153(153 159 159 161) sts.

Work as follows in st.st.
1st row: with black yarn P54(54 56 56 56) sts, P2togtbl, P1 (this is the marked st.), P2tog, P94(94 98 98 100) sts.

2nd row: with black yarn K93(93 97 97 99), K2tog, K1, K2togtbl, K53(53 55 55 55) sts.

Change to red yarn, and cont. in the same way in st.st. losing 2 sts. at centre front on every row, keeping the centre st. straight, and working the foll. colour sequence: 4 rows red, 2 rows white, 3 rows brown. 131(131 137 137 139) sts.

Change to white. Work in K1 P1 rib beginning K, ending 2 sts. before centre st., K2tog, P1, K2togtbl, work in P1 K1 rib to end.
Next row: Rib to 2 sts. before centre st., P2togtbl, K1, P2tog, rib to end.
Cont. in this way, keeping rib correct and dec. 1 st. on either side of centre st. on every row, and also keeping centre st. correct.
Work a total of 8 rows of rib, then cast off in rib, and dec 1 st. on either side of centre st. on this row also.

To make up

Do not press. Join carefully all rem. seams in back stitch.

SCARF ☆

The whole idea of a book of patterns based on *Doctor Who* grew, rather like the scarf itself must have grown, from this piece of knitting which, for many people symbolises the programme. Everyone, from serious devotees of *Doctor Who* to people who have rarely watched, is familiar with Tom Baker's flamboyant, seemingly endless, striped scarf. Because it is so easy to knit, the scarf is an ideal beginner's project, so turn to the How-to-Knit section, page 7, and begin! It is in simple garter stitch and totally unshaped, so the only things you need the pattern for are the colour sequence, the number of stitches to cast on, and when to stop!

You can use any yarn you want to, and make the scarf any size you wish. Remember to use the same thickness of yarn throughout, though, or your scarf will have wavy edges. If you especially want to use a thinner yarn, try knitting two threads of it at once.

This Doctor Who scarf is in chunky yarn, with a typical tension or gauge of 7 stitches per 2 inches (5cm). If you would like to use a finer yarn, you will need to cast on proportionately more, of course, to achieve the same width. Remember a thinner yarn will take ages longer to knit. Colour illustration is on page 54.

Materials

In chunky yarn, 3 × 50gm balls of cream; 4 × 50gm balls of dark brown; 3 × 50gm balls of brick; 2 × 50gm balls of beige; 2 × 50gm balls of grey; 2 × 50gm balls of maroon; 2 × 50gm balls of rust. 1 pair of size 3 (6½mm, US size 10) needles.

Notes

1. Always measure the scarf under *slight* tension, as it will 'drop' and become longer when finished.

2. Work the colour change rows onto the same side so that the scarf has a wrong side. To do this, always join in all new colours at the same edge of the scarf.

Tension

14 sts. and 20 rows = 4in (10cm) on size 3 (6½mm, US size 10) needles in st.st. The whole scarf is worked in garter stitch i.e. all K throughout.

Measurements

Approx. 12 in (30cm) wide and 124in (315cm) long.

To make

Using grey, cast on 42 sts.

Work the following colour sequence in garter stitch (every row K): 4in (10cm) grey, 1in (2½cm) cream, 1in (2½cm) maroon, 4in (10cm) dark brown, 2in (5cm) beige, 1½in (4cm) grey, 2½in (6½cm) rust, 8in (20cm) brick, 2in (5cm) beige, 2in (5cm) cream, 2in (5cm) maroon, 1½in (4cm) rust, 2in (5cm) grey, 1½in (4cm) brick, 4in (10cm) cream, 2in (5cm) maroon, 9in (22½cm) dark brown, 2in (5cm) rust, 2in (5cm) grey, 3in (7½cm) cream, 9in (22½cm) brick, 2in (5cm) cream, 2in (5cm) maroon, 8in (20cm) cream, 2in (5cm) rust, 2in (5cm) grey, 2in (5cm) beige, 9in (22½cm) dark brown, 2in (5cm) maroon, 2in (5cm) dark brown, 4in (10cm) rust, 6in (15cm) cream, 2in (5cm) beige, 3in (7½cm) dark brown, 2in (5cm) maroon, 3in (7½cm) rust, 2in (5cm) beige, 3in (7½cm) dark brown, cast off!

To fringe the scarf:
Cut about 20 pieces of yarn in each of the seven colours, all about 12in (30cm) long. Push a large crochet hook through the scarf from front to back, one row away from the end and behind the edge stitch. Take three of the 12in (30cm) lengths of yarn together and double them in the middle to form a loop. Place these looped threads together over the hook and pull them through to the front of the scarf. Pass all six fringe ends through the loop and pull them tight. Repeat this with further bunches of three pieces of yarn chosen at random from the seven colours, and do so in every alternate stitch of the first row away from the edge. Trim any extra long ends.

NYSSA'S JACKET ☆ ☆ ☆

Nyssa met up with the Doctor on Traken when the Master caused various nasty things to happen to her father, Consul Tremas. She later became a charming and clever, but innocent, companion to both Tom Baker's and Peter Davison's regenerations of the Doctor.

She first wore a delightful wine brown outfit, the top of which provided the inspiration for this jacket. It is not very easy to knit, because it is an unusual shape, with its leg-o'-mutton sleeves – which are, incidentally, very long in a rather medieval way – and its fitted bodice. The fronts meet almost edge to edge and curve away at the collar and hem, and it really does have hems not welts. The pale brown areas are actually randomly placed. One sleeve on the garment shown here has three areas of colour, and the other sleeve has only one. You can place them wherever you wish, but if you prefer to follow a pattern, charts are given for guidance (pages 44–8).

Tension is very important with this garment because the bodice is fitted and also because the sleeves are already very full and a sloppy tension would make them even bigger and therefore difficult to set into the armholes. So do test your tension before you begin. If you are unsure of the best way to do this, refer to the How-to-Knit section on page 7. Colour illustration is on page 42.

Materials
About 8(8 9 9) × 50gm balls of rich dark brown double knitting yarn; 3(3 3 3) × 50gm balls of pale brown double knitting; 5 matching brown buttons; 4 large press-stud fasteners suitable for use with knitting.

Measurements
To fit chest/bust 32(34 36 38)in, 81(86 91 97)cm. Back length 23in (58cm) excluding collar. Sleeve length underarm 19½in (49cm).

Tension
24 sts. and 32 rows = 4in (10cm) on size 8 (4mm, US size 5) needles in st.st.

To make
The garment is made in st.st. throughout except where otherwise stated. The basic pattern is made throughout in dark brown, with pale brown areas worked in each piece as shown on the chart allowing them to run out at the end of the work if your pieces are longer or shorter.

Back
In dark brown, working pale brown areas from the chart, cast on 82(88 94 100) sts.

1st row: K.
2nd row: P.
3rd row: K, inc. 1 st. at either end. (84 90 96 102 sts.)
4th and 5th rows: P.

Cont. in st.st., starting P, and dec. 1 st. each end of the next K row, then every foll. 4th row to 72(78 84 90) sts.

Work straight to a total of 4½in (11½cm) ending after a P row. Mark this row.

Cont. in st.st., working in the pale areas as shown, and inc. 1 st. at each end of the foll. 3rd. then every foll. 5th row to 102(108 114 120) sts.

Work straight to a total measurement of 14in (36cm) or required length.

To shape armholes:
Cast off 5 sts. at beg. of next 2 rows, then dec. 1 st. each end of every foll. alt. row to 78(84 90 96) sts.

Work straight until armhole measures 8in (20cm).

To shape shoulders:
Cast off 7(8 8 9) sts. at beg. of next 6 rows.
Leave rem. 36(36 42 42) sts. on a holder.

Right front

In dark brown, working pale brown areas from chart, cast on 31(34 37 40) sts.

1st row: K.
2nd row: P to last 2 sts., P2tog.
3rd row: K2tog, K to last st., inc. 1 in last st.
4th and 5th rows: P. (30 33 36 39 sts.)
6th row: P.
7th row: Cast on 5 sts. and work these 5 sts. K1, P1, K1, P1, K1, then K to last 2 sts., K2tog.
8th row: P. to last 6 sts., inc. 1 in next st., P1, K1, P1, K1, P1.
9th row: K1, P1, K1, P1, K1, then K to end.
10th row: As 8th row.
11th row: K1, P1, K1, P1, K1, then K to last 2 sts., K2tog.

Repeat rows 8 to 11, losing 1 st. on every 4th row on the outside(armhole edge), and gaining 1 st. on every other row on the inside, but keeping the rib stitches correct, until there are 41(44 47 50) sts.

BBC

Then work straight, keeping rib correct, to end with a P row which matches the marked P row on the back, mark this row.

(**) Keeping rib correct on front edge, and keeping this edge straight throughout, inc. 1 st. at other (armhole) edge on foll. 3rd then every foll. 5th row to 56(59 62 65) sts.

Work straight until front measures same as back to armholes, ending at armhole edge.

Cast off 5 sts. at beg. of next row, then dec. 1 st. at armhole edge of every alt. row to 44(47 50 53) sts.

Work straight until armhole measures 4½in (11cm) ending at neck edge.

Next row: Rib 5 and place these sts. on a pin, cast off 6(6 8 8) sts., work to end.

Keeping armhole straight, dec. 1 st. at neck edge only on next 6(6 7 7) rows, then on every alt. row 6 times.

Work straight until armhole measures same as back to shoulder, ending at shoulder edge.

Cast off 7(8 8 9) sts. at beg. of next and next alt. row.

Work 1 row.

Cast off rem. 7(8 8 9) sts.

Left front

In dark brown, working pale areas from chart, cast on 31(34 37 40) sts.
1st row: K.
2nd row: P2tog, P to end.
3rd row: Inc. 1 st. in first st., K to last 2, K2tog. (30 33 36 39 sts.)
4th and 5th row: P.
6th row: Cast on 5 sts., P to end.
7th row: K2tog, K to last 5, K1, P1, K1, P1, K1.
8th row: P1, K1, P1, K1, P1, inc. 1 P st. in next st., P to end.
9th row: K to last 5, K1, P1, K1, P1, K1.
10th row: As 8th row.
11th row: K2tog, K to last 5, K1, P1, K1, P1, K1.

Repeat rows 8 to 11, losing 1 st. on every 4th row on the outside (armhole) edge, and gaining 1 st. on the inside, but keeping the rib sts. correct, until there are 41(44 47 50) sts.

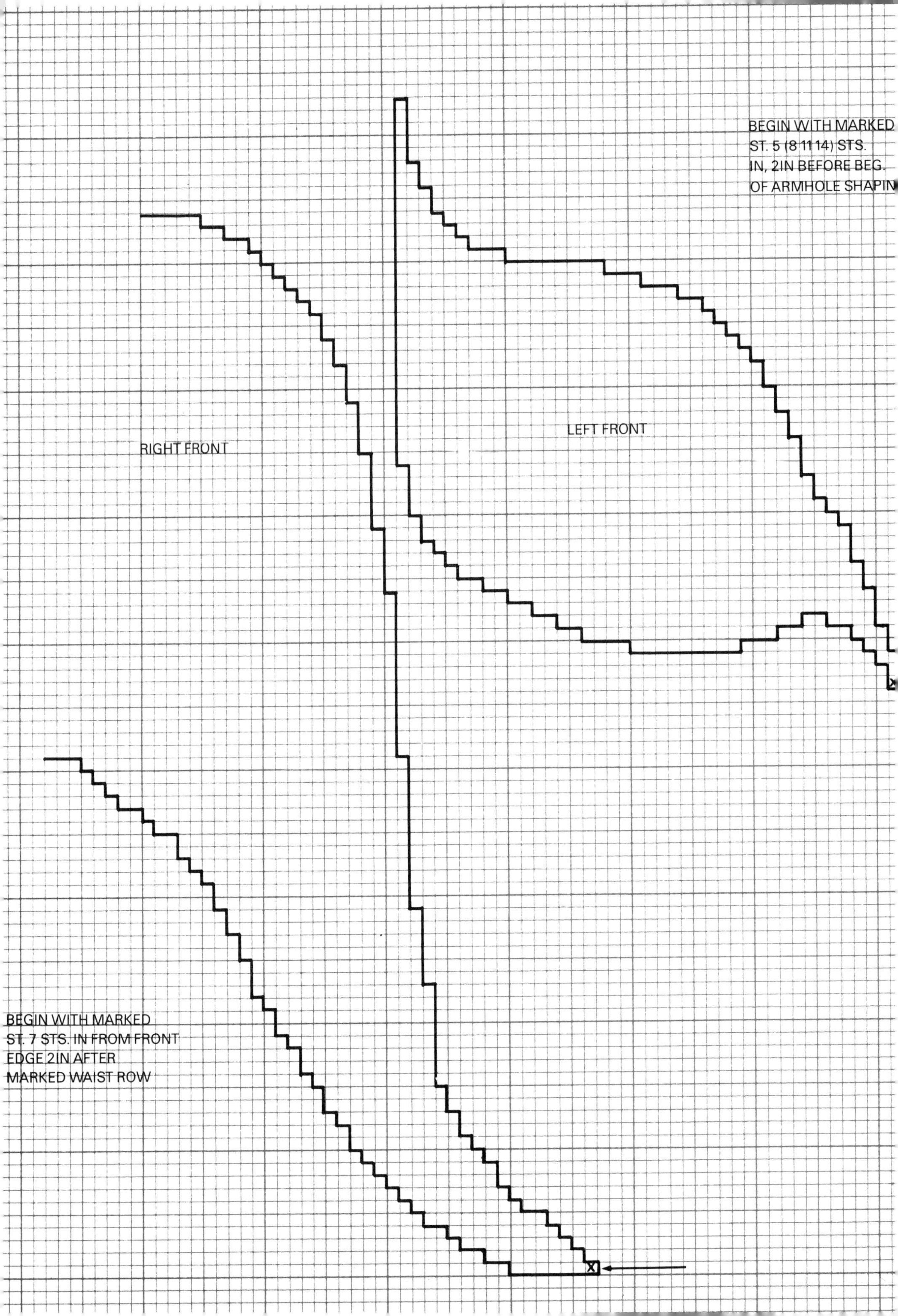
BEGIN WITH MARKED
ST. 5 (8 11 14) STS.
IN, 2IN BEFORE BEG.
OF ARMHOLE SHAPIN
LEFT FRONT
RIGHT FRONT
X
BEGIN WITH MARKED
ST. 7 STS. IN FROM FRONT
EDGE 2IN AFTER
MARKED WAIST ROW
X

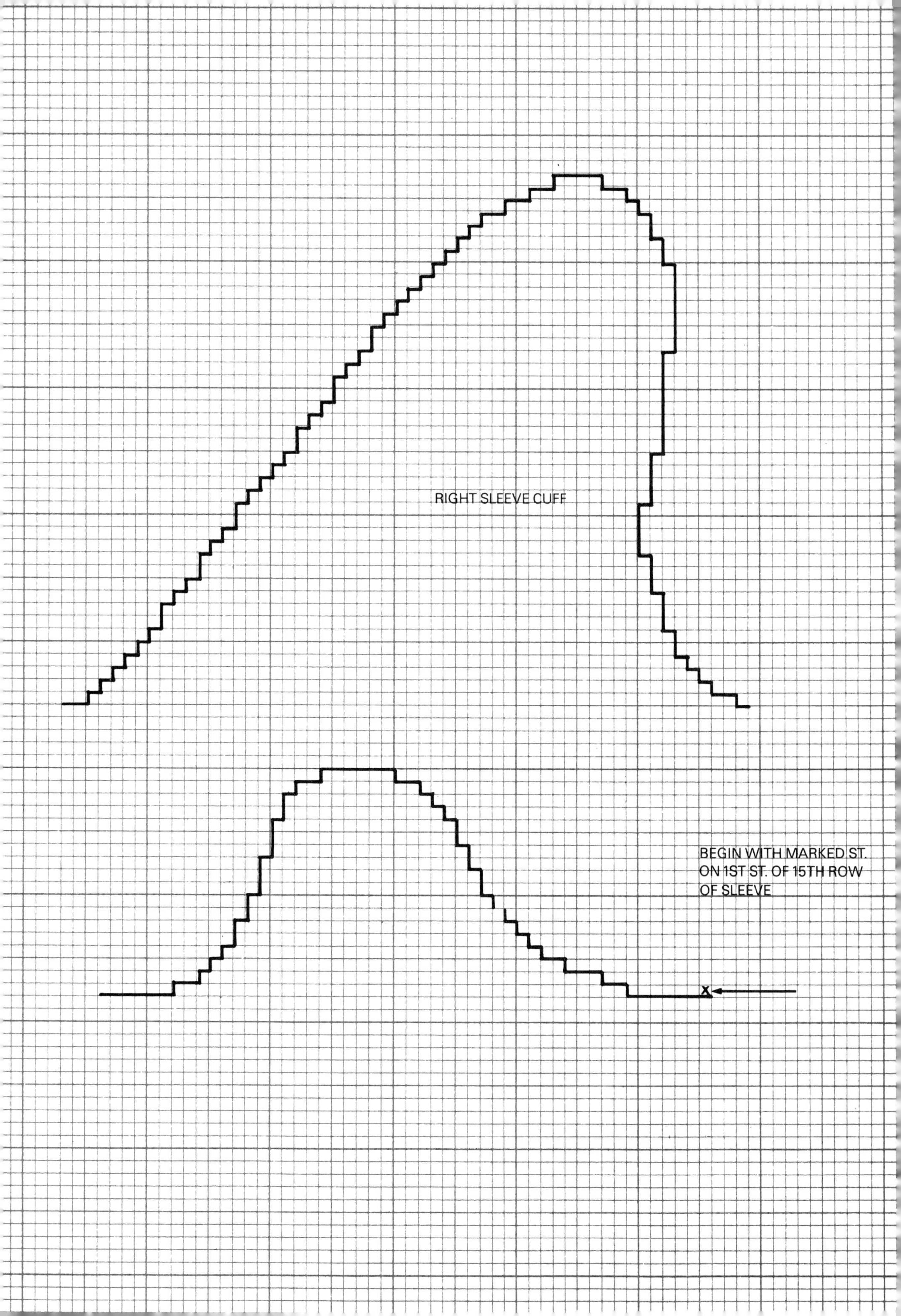
RIGHT SLEEVE CUFF
BEGIN WITH MARKED ST. ON 1ST ST. OF 15TH ROW OF SLEEVE
X

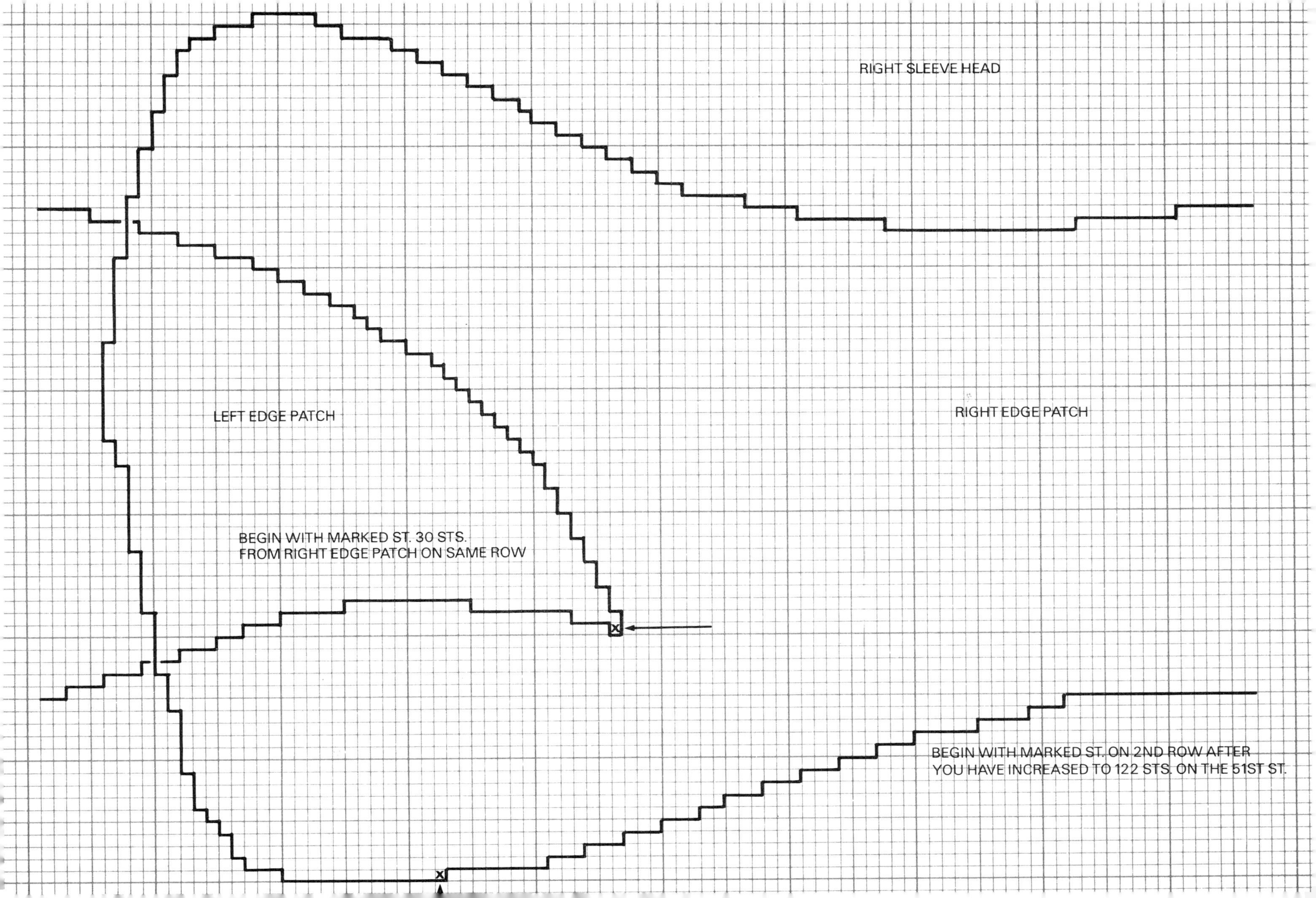
RIGHT SLEEVE HEAD
LEFT EDGE PATCH
RIGHT EDGE PATCH
BEGIN WITH MARKED ST. 30 STS.
FROM RIGHT EDGE PATCH ON SAME ROW
BEGIN WITH MARKED ST. ON 2ND ROW AFTER
YOU HAVE INCREASED TO 122 STS. ON THE 51ST ST.

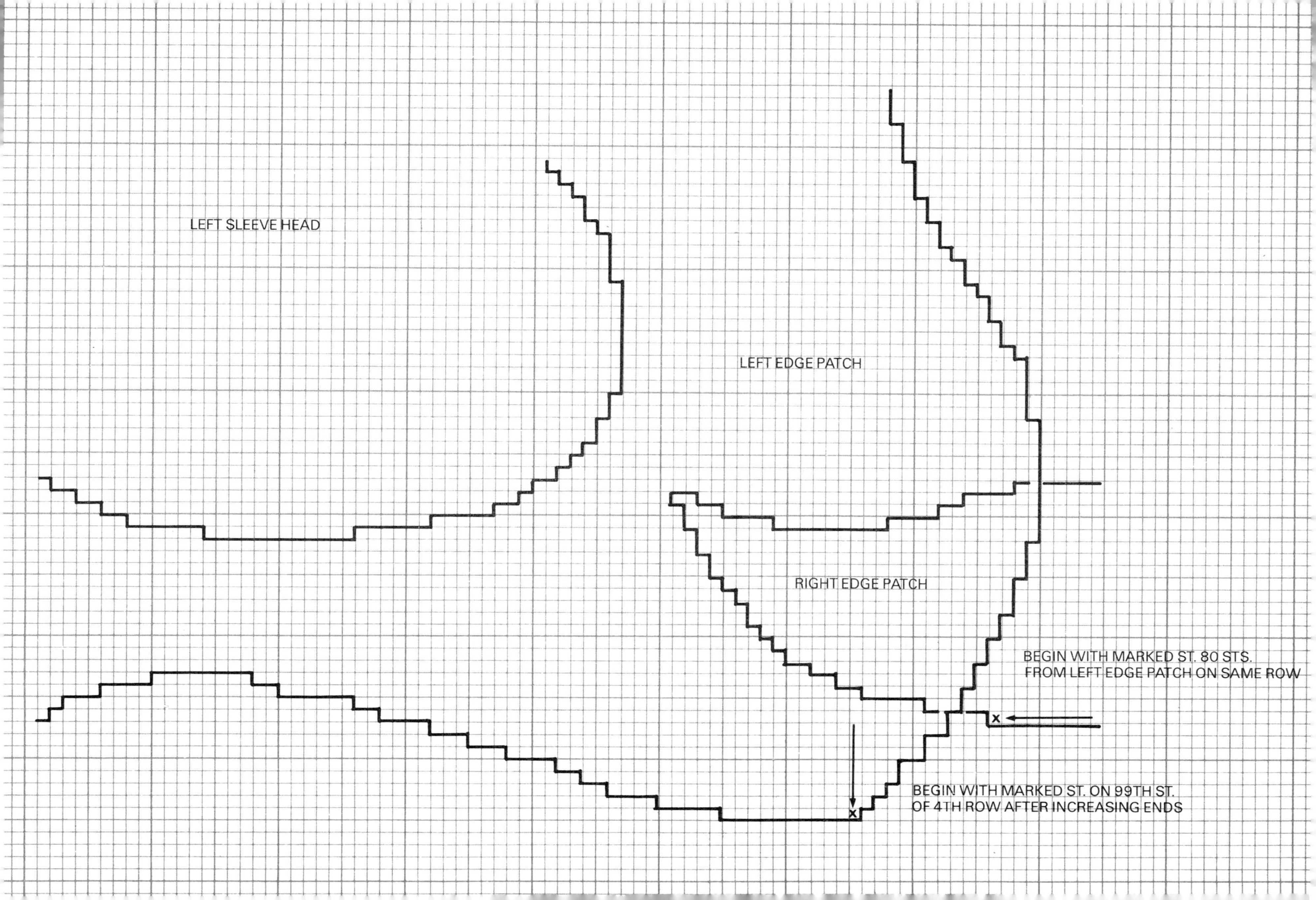
LEFT SLEEVE HEAD
LEFT EDGE PATCH
RIGHT EDGE PATCH
BEGIN WITH MARKED ST. 80 STS.
FROM LEFT EDGE PATCH ON SAME ROW
BEGIN WITH MARKED ST. ON 99TH ST.
OF 4TH ROW AFTER INCREASING ENDS

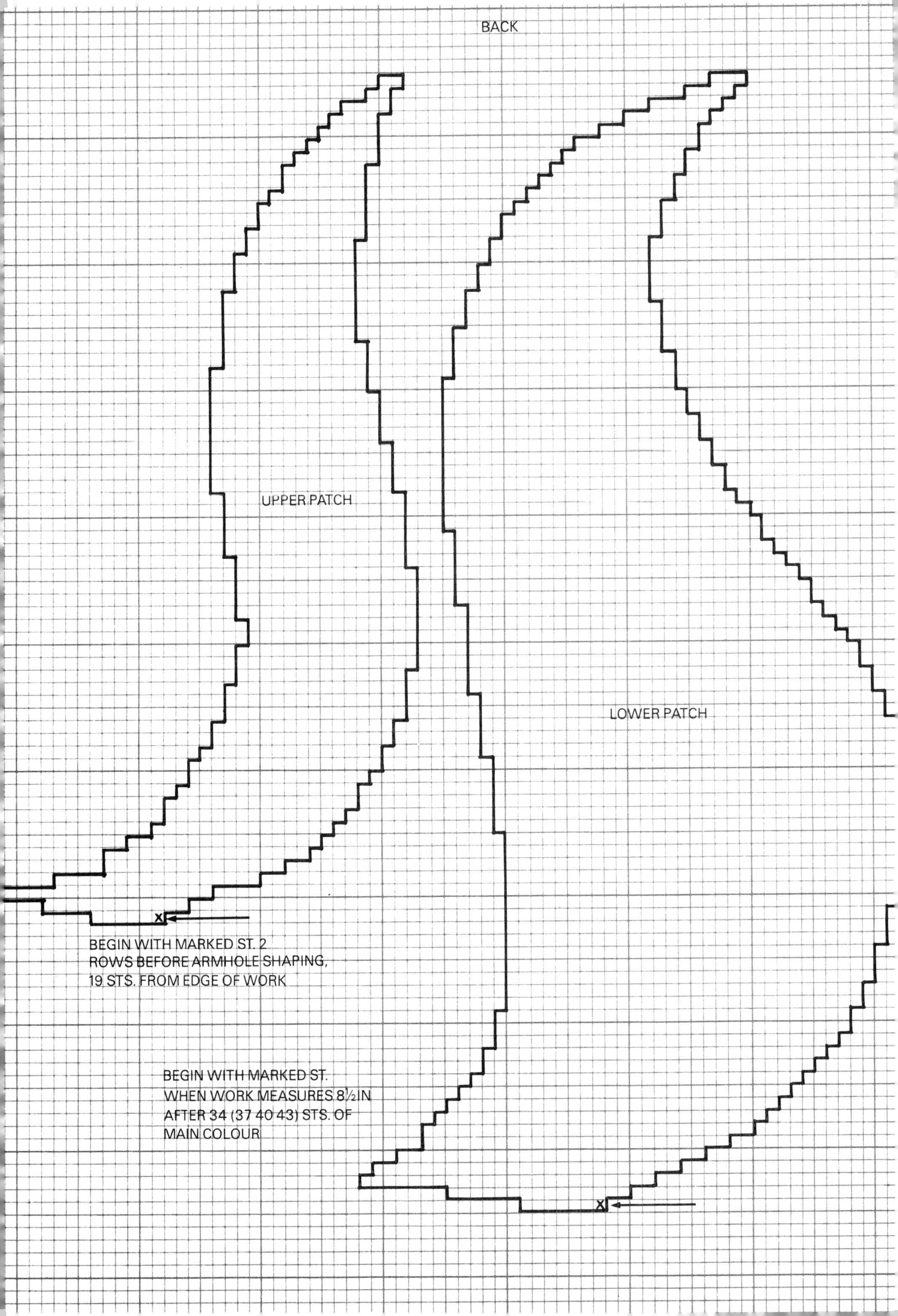
BACK
UPPER PATCH
LOWER PATCH
x
BEGIN WITH MARKED ST. 2
ROWS BEFORE ARMHOLE SHAPING,
19 STS. FROM EDGE OF WORK
x
BEGIN WITH MARKED ST.
WHEN WORK MEASURES 8½IN
AFTER 34 (37 40 43) STS. OF
MAIN COLOUR

Work straight, keeping rib correct, ending with a P row which matches the marked P row on the right front, mark this row.

Work as for right front as from (**).

Sleeves

Both alike in shaping, but with different pale brown areas, (see charts). Cast on 48 sts. and work 4 rows in st.st. beg. with a K row.
5th row: P.

Cont. in st.st. for 4 rows beg. P.

Inc. 1 st. each end of next and every foll. 9th row to 66 sts. ending with a P row to make the next row K.

Next row: Inc. 1 st. in first st., K31, (inc. 1 st. in next st.) twice, K31, inc. 1 st. in last st.
Work 3 rows.
Next row: Inc. 1 st. in first st., K33, (inc. 1 st. in next st.) twice, K33, inc. 1 st. in last st.
Work 3 rows.

Cont. in this way, increasing by 4 sts. on every 4th row to 162 sts. and marking the work when it is 20in (51cm) long.

Work straight to a total length of 25½in (65cm).

Cast off 5 sts. at the beg. of every row to 17 sts.

Work 1 row, then cast off.

Collar

Carefully join both shoulder seams. Using needles one size smaller than for main tension, with right side facing, pick up and cont. to rib the 5 sts. left on a pin at the top of the right front, pick up and K21(21 25 25) sts. around and up the right front neck, the 36(36 42 42) sts. left at the back neck, *knitting the two centre sts. together,* and 21(21 25 25) sts. down the left front. Then rib the 5 sts. left on a pin at the left front. (87 87 101 101 sts.)

Keeping 5 sts. in rib at either end, from now on, work the centre 77(77 91 91) sts. in moss st. i.e.:
1st row: (K1, P1) repeat throughout to end.
2nd row: P1, K1, P1, K1, P1, (P1, K1) repeat to last 6 sts., P2, K1, P1, K1, P1.

Repeat these two rows four more times (i.e. 10 rows), then, keeping rib and moss st. correct throughout, cont. as follows:
Next row: K1, P1, K1, P1, K2togtbl, work in moss st. to last 6 sts., K2tog, P1, K1, P1, K1.
Next row: P1, K1, P1, K1, P2tog, work in moss st. to last 6, P2togtbl, K1, P1, K1, P1.

Repeat these two rows once, then the first row only once more.

Cast off fairly loosely, keeping stitch patterns correct on the casting off row, and working the 5th and 6th sts. in, at either end, together as before (by P2tog and P2togtbl as above).

Making up
Press according to instructions on the yarn band. Make up side seams, matching marked rows at waist, and sleeve seams from cuff to point marked when sleeve was 20in (51cm) long. The remaining straight sleeve edges fit into the armhole. Turn cuff and bottom edge hems onto the wrong side and slip stitch into place. Insert the sleeves into the armhole, matching underarm seams and stitching about 3in (7½cm) on either side of the seam without gathering. Gather the remainder of the sleeve top and ease evenly into the armhole. Sew buttons about 1½in (4cm) in from the edge of the left front at the bottom of the collar, at the waist, and then space the other three buttons evenly between, also the same distance from the edge. Make loops with twisted cords or plaits and attach to the inside of the right front so that the loops stretch firmly over the buttons when the two ribbed edges are overlapped. Invisibly sew on press-studs to close the right front over the left, stitching these onto the ribbed edge strip, and spacing them between the buttons.

ROMANA'S T-SHIRT ☆☆

Romana was one of the Doctor's companions for two years and wore, for some of her many episodes, a delightful Edwardian-style sailor suit. Nautical fashions have always been popular so, for your own version, you can wear either the 4-ply striped T-shirt patterned here, or Romana's sailor top in fabric (see page 59 and pattern on page 107), or both. The T-shirt would look very good in other colours too, especially red and white, or you could knit it in a single colour.

It is much easier when knitting stripes to carry the unused yarn fairly loosely up the side and loop it in every other row until it is needed. This is much easier than joining the yarn every time and far less messy than breaking the colour off and dealing with masses of ends. Colour illustration is on pages 52–3.

Sizes
To fit chest/bust 28(30 32 34 36 38) in, 71(76 81 86 91 97) cm.

Materials
3(3 4 4 4 4) × 50gm balls of 4 ply yarn in white; 1(1 1 2 2 2) × 50gm ball(s) in blue.

Tension
28 sts. and 36 rows = 4in (10cm) in st.st. on size 10 (3¼mm, US size 3) needles.

Back
Using size 12 (2½mm, US size 1) needles and white, cast on 107(113 121 129 135 143) sts.
1st row: K1, *P1, K1, rep. from * to end.
2nd row: P1, *K1, P1, rep. from * to end.
Rep. these 2 rows until 2in (5cm) of rib has been worked.

Change to size 10 (3¼mm, US size 3) needles, and cont. in st.st. working stripe pattern 8 rows white, 2 rows blue, repeated throughout, until work measures 11(12 13 15 15½ 16)in, 28(30 33 38 39 41)cm, or required length to armhole(**).

To shape armhole:
Keeping stripe pattern correct, cast off 4(5 5 6 6 7) sts. at beg. of next 2 rows.
Dec. 1 st. each end of next 5(5 7 7 7 7) rows, then every alt. row until 83(87 91 95 99 103) sts. remain*.
Work straight until armholes measure 6(6 7 7 7½ 8) in, 15(15 18 18 19 20)cm.

To shape shoulders:
Cast off 6(7 7 6 6 6) sts. at beg. of next 6(6 6 8 8 8) rows, then 7(5 6 5 6 7) sts. at beg. of foll. 2 rows. Slip rem. 33(35 37 37 39 41) sts. onto a holder.

Front

Work as for back as far as * matching stripe pattern throughout.
Work straight until armholes measure 4(4 4½ 4½ 5 5) in, 10(10 11½ 11½ 12½ 12½) cm.

To shape neck:
Work 31(33 35 37 39 40) sts., turn and cont. to work this side first.
◊Dec. 1 st. at neck edge on next 3(5 5 5 5 5) rows, then every alt. row until 25(26 27 29 30 31) sts. remain. Work straight until armhole measures the same as on the back, ending at armhole edge.
Cast off 6(7 7 6 6 6) sts. at beg of next, then every alt. row until 7(5 6 5 6 7) sts. remain.
Work 1 row.
Cast off ◊.
Place centre 21(21 21 21 21 23) sts. on a holder.
Rejoin yarn to rem. 31(33 35 37 39 40) sts. and shape in the same way as for the first side, from ◊ to ◊.

Sleeves

Using size 12 (2½mm, US size 1) needles, and white, cast on 79(83 87 91 95 101) sts. and work 1in (2½cm) in K1P1 rib in the same way as for the back.

Change to size 10 (3¼mm, US size 3) and cont. in st.st. working stripes as for back to a total length of 5(5½ 6 6 6½ 6½) in, 12½(14 15 15 16½ 16½) cm, or required length, ending at the same point in the stripe pattern as on the front and back at **.
Cast off 4(5 5 6 6 7) sts. at beg. of next 2 rows.
Dec. 1 st. at each end of next 3 rows, then every alt. row until 45(43 43 39 39 41) sts. remain.
Dec. 1 st. at each end of next 5 rows.
Cast off 8(7 7 5 5 6) sts. at beg. of foll. 2 rows.
Cast off rem. 19 sts.

Neckband

Join left shoulder seam.
Using size 12 (2½mm, US size 1) needles and white yarn, with right side of work facing, pick up and K onto wrong side 33(35 37 37 39 41) sts. on holder at back neck, working 2tog in centre, 23(25 27 31 31 33) sts. down left side of front neck, 21(21 21 21 21 23) sts. on holder at front neck, and 23(25 27 31 31 33) sts. up right side of front neck. Work 8 rows in K1P1 rib in the same way as for the back.
Cast off loosely in rib.

Making up

Press according to instructions on yarn band and join all seams, matching the stripe pattern as far as possible.

ADRIC'S TUNIC ☆ ☆

Adric was a young companion from the planet Alzarius, who became very popular during the series, before he died helping to save the Earth from an attack by the Cybermen. During his time with the Doctor, he wore some splendid clothes, two of which are adapted here in this tunic and on page 65 as an anorak. The tunic is designed to be worn over a shirt as it has a tied edge-to-edge fitting, and is in one multisize to fit children of up to about twelve years old. It can be worn complete with the string belt to give an authentic Alzarian feel, or with any belt you choose! Adric was given the star pin as an award, and the instructions to make it are also given. Colour illustration is on page 41, sewing pattern on page 106.

Materials

1½yd (1.35m) of yellow cotton fabric 45in (114cm) wide; ¼yd (25cm) of red cotton fabric 45in (114cm) wide; piece of quilting wadding approximately 15in × 6in (37½cm × 15cm); several yards or metres of tweed, or rough yarn, or even string (depending on the thickness); thin card; blue and gold enamel paint; glue; safety-pin; and adhesive tape.

Measurements

Actual chest measurement of garment 31in (79cm). Armhole depth 7½in (19cm). Back length 23in (58cm).

To make

1. In yellow fabric, cut one back, two fronts, two front facings, one back neck facing and two armhole facings. Keep yellow scraps for bias strips (see 10 below). In red fabric, cut one pocket and one trim strip. In wadding, cut two pieces the same shape as the armhole facing but *without* any turning allowances.

2. With right sides together, join shoulder and side seams.

3. With right sides together, seam and two front facings to the ends of the back neck facing so forming a facing for the complete front and neck opening.

4. With right sides together, stitch this completed facing in around the outside edge of the front and neck opening. Clip seam allowances if necessary, and turn on to the wrong side. Neaten facing edges if required.

5. With right sides together, seam armhole facing into a tube, then seam into the armhole. Turn onto the wrong side. Neaten facing edges if required.

6. Insert the wadding between the armhole facing and the main garment. Tack or

pin into place then machine around the armhole through the wadding and both layers of fabric, in three lines which are approximately ¾in, 1¾in and 2½in (2cm, 4½cm and 6½cm) away from the edge – so quilting the armhole.

7. Turn onto the wrong side and machine a small hem all round the bottom of the garment.

8. Hem one long edge and both short edges of the red strip. Neaten the remaining edge if required.

9. Place the red strip right side up under the bottom edge of the garment with 3in (7½cm) of red showing and, beginning at the left front edge, machine this strip in yellow, at its top edge all round the garment, stitching line shown. Turning any excess onto the wrong side at the right front edge, making a fold inside this front edge.

10. From scrap fabric, cut, joining if necessary, six bias or straight-cut strips, as preferred, each 1in (2½cm) wide and approximately 14in (35cm) long. Turn their long edges in by ¼in (½cm) then double them, so forming neatened strips ¼in (½cm) wide. Machine these along their length. Attach in pairs as ties at either side of the front opening: one pair at the top, one pair immediately below the curve, and one 6in (15cm) below that.

11. Neaten the pocket on all four sides and attach where shown.

12. Cut a star shape (pattern on page 116), in card, and paint with blue enamel paint. Cut another, a fraction larger all round, and paint its edges gold. Stick the blue star over the gold one so that the gold edges show. Attach a pin with adhesive tape to the back, and pin to the pocket.

13. Make a twisted cord or plait in the yarn or string, long enough to go twice around waist and tie.

ROMANA'S SAILOR TOP ☆☆

Lady Romanadvoratrelundar, usually known as Romana, is herself a Time Lord and has appeared in the series in two regenerations. In the second, she appeared in the sort of costume that young people many decades ago use to sport on the beach. Made very popular in Victorian times, the sailor suit or blouse, or just a sailor 'look', has proved to have remarkable staying power, occurring again and again in fashion, right up to today. This sailor top is designed to be used on top of the knitted T-shirt on page 55, which is the way Romana wore it, but it is generously cut and can be worn over blouses, dresses or even jumpers if you wish. There is no reason why it shouldn't be any colour you like, although traditionally sailor suits are navy – logically enough – and, for the authentic look, white and red trim are used here. The three sizes (sewing pattern page 107) fit from young teens through the middle women's sizes, and the shirt fits over the head with no openings. Colour illustration is on page 52.

Materials

2¼yds (2m) of navy blue cotton 45in (114cm) wide; about 60in (150cm) of white cotton braid 1in (2½cm) wide. About 1½yds (135cm) of wide bright red satin ribbon.

Measurements

To fit chest sizes 28–30, 32–34, and 36–38in [(in cm) 71–76, 81–86, 91–97], with an actual measurement around under the arms of 32in, 36in and 40in (81cm, 91cm and 102cm). The sleeves have an underarm measurement of 16in, 17in and 18in (41cm, 43cm and 46cm) respectively.

To make

1. Cut out one back, one front, two collars, two sleeves, two pockets and a bias strip, joined if necessary, 2½in × 17½in (6½cm × 44cm).

2. With right sides together, make the side and shoulder seams and make the long underarm seam of the sleeve.

3. With right sides together, insert and stitch in the sleeves.

4. Hem each pocket along one short side, which then becomes the top edge of the pocket.

5. With the two long side edges turned under, stitch the pockets into position as shown, stitching the long sides only and matching the bottom raw edge of the pocket with the bottom raw edge of the front. Stitch a strengthening square or triangle at the top of the side pocket stitching line to give a strong pocket.

6. Turn under and machine a hem around the whole of the bottom of the garment, so turning under and neatening the bottom of the pockets at the same time.

7. Turn under and machine a hem around the cuff.

8. With right sides together stitch the two collar pieces together around the two long side edges and across the back, leaving the neck opening edges raw.

9. Turn the collar, trimming and clipping seam allowances if necessary.

10. Tack or pin the collar into position round the outside (i.e. the right side) of the garment's neck line, matching all raw edges.

11. With right sides together pin or tack the bias strip over the collar, also on the right side and again with all raw edges matching.

12. Machine around the neck edge through all these four thicknesses of fabric.

13. Turn the bias strip onto the wrong side and tack it down so that the collar, caught between the bias strip and the main garment will lie flat over the shoulders. Run a line of machining immediately inside the neck edge to catch the bias strip on to the wrong side, making sure that the machining line does not catch the collar which lies free on the shoulders. Neaten the long edge of the bias strip if required and neaten the ends together inside the bottom of the V-neck.

14. Stitch the white braid all round the extreme edge of the collar on the right side, keeping the corners square, and neatening the ends of the braid against the ends of the bias strip inside the front V of the neck.

15. Place the red ribbon centrally under the collar and tie it in a soft neck tie-knot loosely below the V. Neaten the ends of the ribbon if neccessary, and, if desired, stitch it in place at the centre back neck.

TEGAN'S BOOB TUBE ☆

When Tegan Jovanka, an Australian air-hostess, inadvertently stumbled upon the TARDIS, she became a favourite companion – in spite of, or perhaps because of, frequently losing her temper whenever things go wrong. Among her very glamorous clothes is this 'boob-tube' which is made here of plain white fabric trimmed with broderie anglaise strip, but which could be made in any fabric, lace or not, and could also very easily be given straps, made with plain strips of fabric or ribbon. Because the top opens down the back, the straps could simply be fixed front and back, but, if you wished, you could attach two lengths of ribbon for each strap and tie a bow on the shoulder. The boob tube is very easy to make, and would be an ideal project for a beginner, perhaps with a little help from her friends? Sewing pattern is on page 108.

Materials

¾yd (0.75m) of plain white fabric, 45in (114cm) wide; 40in (1m) of 3½in (9cm) wide broderie anglaise or lace trim; about 24in (60cm) of white elastic (unstretched); 9½in (25cm) of Velcro or similar press-strip-fastening, or buttons or press-studs.

Measurements

To fit 34, 36 or 38in (86, 91 or 97cm) bust. Length at front 12in (30cm).

To make

1. Cut out one front and two backs, one the reverse of the other in plain white.

2. Stitch all the darts closed on the wrong side.

3. With right sides together, join both side seams.

4. Make a channel for the elastic by folding down, as shown, all along the top, and hemming and stitching down the raw edge.

5. Attach the broderie anglaise trim on the right side all round the stitch line shown, so that it just covers the top edge.

6. Measure off a comfortable length of elastic to fit the wearer at underarm. Thread this length through the channel and secure about 1in (2½cm) from each end with a pin or a tacking stitch.

7. Neaten the bottom edge all round.

8. On the right back, turn all raw edges over on to the *right* side down the whole

opening edge. Cut the Velcro to fit the length of this opening edge, peel it apart, and firmly machine one piece of it on, at the edge, on the right side, over all these raw edges, taking care to catch firmly the end of the elastic.

9. On the left back, turn all raw edges over on to the *wrong* side and stitch the other piece of Velcro on in the same way, but on the wrong side, again being sure to catch the elastic. Ensure that the two pieces of Velcro match and close the back of the garment neatly.

10. On this boob tube Velcro really behaves best but, if you prefer, you could use buttons and button-holes, mock buttons over press-studs or press-studs on their own. If you choose not to use Velcro, then, before doing buttons or press-studs, turn all the raw edges on to the wrong sides and neaten with a strip of white ribbon or tape sewn on in the same way as for the Velcro, on the wrong side, which also gives these fastenings strength, and gives a double fabric layer for button-holes.

DOCTOR WHO

ADRIC'S ANORAK ☆☆

In 'Four to Doomsday', when the forces of good are lined up against the evil Urbankans, Adric wears a splendid black space-suit trimmed with quilted silver. There is not much call yet for space-suits in ordinary wear, but the top half of the suit converts readily into a spectacular anorak jacket which makes any lad look like Adric. You can of course use other colours and, if you are making it for a biker, why not trim it with reflective ribbon so that he, or she, will be seen at night.

The anorak is generously cut to fit boys or girls up to mid teens, although for older wearers you may need to add to the sleeve length. In order to do this, or to shorten the sleeve length for that matter, when drawing the pattern out onto your squared paper, lengthen or shorten the sleeve pattern midway between the bottom of the armhole and the cuff, straightening the cutting lines between these two points. Sewing pattern is on page 109, colour illustration on page 51.

The anorak is fastened at the waist, cuff and neck with Velcro, or similar press-strip-fastening, but you can if you wish, easily use button-holes or press-studs as the fabric is double at these points.

Materials

2¼yd (2m) of suitable main fabric e.g. strong cotton, waterproof material, or any smooth firm but not too thick fabric, preferably washable, 45in (114cm) wide; 4yd (3¾m) of 1¼in (3½cm) wide washable silver braid; approximately 18in (½m) of strong elastic; a piece of interfacing about 10½in × 4in (27cm × 10cm), but if the fabric/braid are very stiff this is not needed; 4in (10cm) of Velcro or similar press-strip-fastening, or four spot-fasteners in Velcro; 19½in (49cm) silver or black open-ended medium weight zip-fastener.

Measurements

Actual garment measurement around at underarm 39in (99cm). Back neck length 23in (58cm). Underarm 17in (43cm).

To make

1. Cut out, in plain main material, one back, two fronts, one the reverse of the other, two pairs of sleeve halves, each pair the reverse of the other, and two of each of the following pieces; front facing, one the reverse of the other; collar; cuff; pocket and tab. If required, cut out two pieces of cuff interfacing as shown.

2. Place the two halves of the pocket right sides together, and seam the long curved side only.

3. Place the right front and the back right sides together and seam the side seam from the armhole to within about 9in (23cm) of the bottom edge, so leaving room for the pocket at the bottom of the seam.

4. Turn the pocket and insert it, in this seam right sides together, with its longer straight edge matching the seam edges, and its shorter straight edge matching the bottom edges. Stitch it in up one longer edge and down the other, so inserting it in the seam and leaving the bottom edge open. Turn it through onto the inside and place it flat against the inside of the right front, pinning it in position.

5. With right sides together make the side seam between the back and left front.

6. Place each pair of sleeve pieces right sides together and seam the longer top edge. Then make the bottom sleeve seam leaving a 3in (7½cm) opening at the cuff end. Neaten the edges of this opening.

7. With right sides together, insert the sleeves into the armholes and seam.

8. Turn back onto the wrong side the seam allowance on the opening edge of each front and each front facing. Place these pieces with their wrong sides together and insert the fabric of each half of the zip between them down each respective side. Machine into place. Neaten facing edges if required.

9. Place the two collar pieces right sides together and stitch all around except for a sufficient opening along one long edge to accommodate the whole of the raw neck edge, so leaving a tab at the top of the left (or right if you prefer) front.

10. Turn the collar right side out and stitch into place, catching in all raw edges of facings and main pieces, and zip tape ends, and turning all seam allowances on to the wrong side.

11. Fold the cuff pieces in half with right sides together, place a piece of interfacing if used, on the wrong side of one half, and seam the two short sides and one long side. Turn.

12. Turn the seam allowance at each side of the sleeve opening onto the wrong side and stitch the cuff into place, leaving a small overlap on the back edge of the opening, and turning all seam allowances onto the wrong side.

13. Make a ¾in (2cm) neatened hem all along the bottom of the garment, catching in the bottom of both facings, the zip tapes and the pocket, and leaving two gaps in your stitching 5in (12½cm) from each of the front edges. Thread the elastic through the hem between these two gaps, after cutting, if neccessary, to a comfortable length for the wearer, and stitch securely at each end.

14. Place the right sides of the two tab pieces together. Seam all but the straight short side, turn, neaten and attach on the left side, or right if you prefer, of the front opening at the bottom.

15. Attach pieces of Velcro, or use your chosen fastening, to close the neck, cuffs and waist tab.

16. Stitch on your chosen braid around the collar, cuffs and upper arms, up the armhole seams, and onto the waist tab.

K9 TOY ☆☆

A cuddly computer? Why not? Certainly K9 has endeared himself to his fans in a way that no other piece of technical wizardry could possibly have done. So now you can make K9 in two squashy forms, one to sit on (see page 98) and this one to take to bed for protection and advice in the night. He still has his data-com probe, his radio signal booster antenna and his tracking sensors, even if they are slightly modified by being made of yarn instead of obscure metal alloys. He even has plenty of buttons to press so that he can be programmed into being a child's companion – maybe he could even be programmed to make the bed in the morning! Will he fit in well with your family? 'AFFIRMATIVE'! Colour illustration is on page 63.

Sizes
15in long (38cm) and 10in high (25cm).

Materials
2 × 50gm balls of double knitting yarn in grey; scraps of double knitting yarn in dark pink, blue and white; scraps of silver yarn; about 500gm washable toy stuffing; about 12in (30cm) tartan ribbon; one large and one small red button; dog tag.

Tension
24 sts. and 32 rows = 4in (10cm) in st.st. on size 8 (4mm, US size 5) needles.

Side pieces
Make two, one the reverse of the other in grey.

Cast on 72 sts.
Working in st.st. beg. with K row, dec. the right-hand side of the work by 1 st. on every 4th row. *At the same time* dec. the left-hand side of the work by 1 st. on every 4th row 6 times, then work 3 more rows.
Dec. at this side on every row 8 times.
Work 16 rows without shaping.
Cast off.

Gusset
Make one in grey.

Cast on 50 sts.
Work 12in (30cm) straight in st.st., and mark this point.
Dec. 1 st. each end of next, then every 4th row to 36 sts.
Dec. 1 st. each end of every 3rd row to 18 sts. Mark this point.

Work 8in (20cm) straight. Mark this point.
Then inc. 1 st. each end of every 3rd row to 50 sts.
Work straight if necessary until length from last marked point equals the length of the front edge of the main piece. (i.e. the edge without a step in.)
Cast off.

Head
Make two, one the reverse of the other in grey.

Cast on 24 sts.
Working in st.st. inc. 1 st. each end of every row to 32 sts.
Keeping left-hand edge (back) straight, cont. to inc. on every row at right-hand edge only to 44 sts.
Work 1 in (2½cm) straight ending at right-hand edge (front).
Cast off 19 sts. at beg of next row.
Work 1½in (4cm) straight.
Dec. 1 st. each end of every row to 21 sts.
Cast off.

Head gusset
Cast on 8 sts. in grey.
Working in st.st. inc. 1 st. each end of every 4th row to 16 sts.
Work straight until work measures 3in (7½cm) ending with a P row.

Change to dark pink and K 1 row.
*Work 3 rows reversed st.st.
Work 3 rows st.st.*
Repeat from * to *.
Work 3 rows reversed st.st.

Change back to grey and work 14in (36cm) in st.st. without shaping.
Dec. 1 st. each end of every 4th row to 8 sts.
Work 10 rows straight.
Cast off.

Radio signal booster antenna (The tail)
Cast on 16 sts. in grey.

Working in st.st. dec. 1 st. each end of every 3rd row to 4 sts.
Work 2 rows.
Run a thread through rem.sts. and leave.

Tracking sensors (The ears)
Make two, both alike.

Work in moss st. throughout in white and silver used together.

Cast on 6 sts.
Work 1 row.
Inc. 1 st. each end of next row.
Work 3 rows.
Dec. 1 st. each end of every row to 4 sts.
Cast off.

Making up

Insert main gusset between two main side pieces, matching marks and noting that the gusset join is at the front of the base. The edge with the step is the back of each side piece. The first marked point matches the back bottom corner of the sides; the second marked point matches the back top corner of the sides; the third marked point matches the front top corner of the sides. Stuff the body. Insert the head gusset between the two head pieces noting that the gusset joins at the top of the front of the nose and the dark pink ridged part of the gusset fits between the two vertical edges at the front of the head pieces. Stuff the head. Stitch on the tracking sensors with the base slightly curved, about 1in ($2\frac{1}{2}$cm) behind the top of the dark pink section.

Stitch the radio signal booster antenna into a cone, stuff and attach at the rear. Swiss darn or duplicate stitch (see how-to section, page 15) 'K9' centrally on the top half of the right side, and the console centrally on the top of the back using the chart. Firmly attach the head. Stitch the ribbon into a collar around the neck. Tie the dog tag to the collar with a silver thread. If it proves difficult to acquire a dog tag, spray or paint a small circle of card in silver, and pierce a hole in it. Stitch the smaller red button over the larger, centrally in the lower half of the dark pink piece on the front of the head to form the retractable (although it isn't of course) data-com probe. For a very small child, you may prefer to embroider these last two details or make them from fabric.

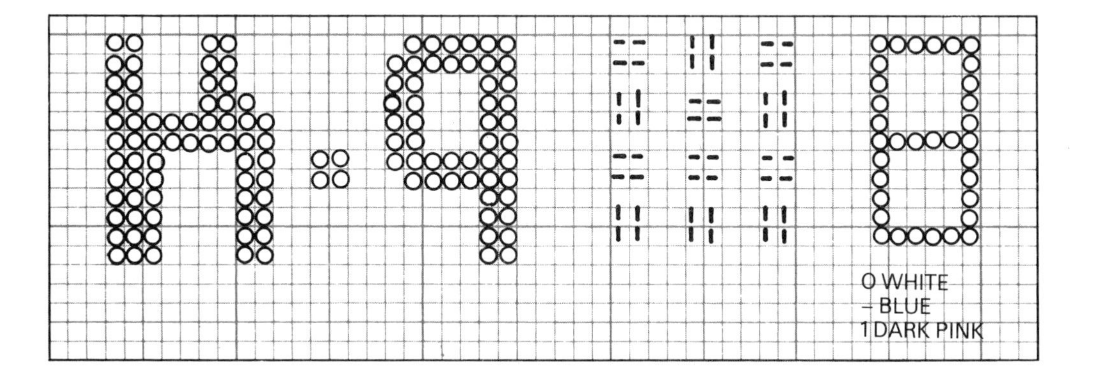

KNIT A NASTY ☆

One of the fascinations of *Doctor Who* throughout the series from the very beginning has been the spectacular collection of aliens and baddies. They range from hi-tech to low life, from massive to microscopic, and from psychological to mind-boggling. It was very hard to choose which of this ghastly gallery to turn into puppets but here is a selection. These are knitted, the ones on page 100 are sewn, and there is a theatre on page 118 in which they can perform perhaps along with the appropriate regeneration of the Doctor (see page 72).

The pattern here is very simple, and can be adapted as the basis for any favourite enemy of the Doctor. The furry ones or squashy ones are best knitted, the metallic or scaly ones are best sewn. Knit the basic pattern in things like green slubby yarn, adding a central eye, to make Scaroth, or in furry yarn to make Yeti or one of the giant spiders from the planet Metebelis III, adding lots of legs of course. See colour illustration on pages 30–1.

BASIC PATTERN

Tension

The puppets are so simple and adaptable that the variations in size caused by different tensions don't really matter. Use the needle most suited to the yarn and to the effect you want to create.

Materials

Each puppet takes about a 50gm ball, but this depends very much on the yarn, and it does not matter if yarns are mixed or if you improvise.

Measurements

Each puppet is about 4½in (11½cm) across the main part and about 8½in (22cm) high, although you can, of course, vary this as much as you wish.

Main pieces

Make two, both alike.
Cast on 22 sts. and K 4 rows.
Change to st.st. or whatever stitch pattern suits your particular monster.
Work straight to a total length of 7in (18cm) or required length.
Dec. 1 st. at each end of next, then every alt. row to 2 sts.
K2tog. then fasten off.

Arms

Make two, both alike.
Cast on 16 sts. and work 2in (5cm) straight in your chosen stitch pattern.
Next row: (Work 2tog) to end.
Next row: As previous row.
Run a thread through the rem. 4 sts.

To make up

Gather the stitches left at the end of the arm using the thread left, and seam the arm with this thread, leaving the cast-on end open. Seam the two halves of the puppet together inserting the arms into the side seams about ½in (1½cm) below the beginning of the shaping. Decorate according to instruction given below, or in any way you wish.

AXON

This particular horrid pile of red 'tree-roots' lumbered on to our screens in 'The Claws of Axos', and makes a splendid glove puppet capable of plenty of animation, in spite of having no discernable face or features.

Make the basic puppet in any rough red or orangey mixture yarn in st.st. To decorate you need a ball of any very lumpy red or reddish brown fashion yarn. Cut this into rough lengths of 10–12in (25–30cm) and knot the lengths at random all over the puppet at about ½in (1½cm) intervals. To knot a length in, thread a piece of the yarn on a blunt-ended sewing needle and make a single stitch with it in the chosen spot. Draw the thread through, leaving a long length, then make another stitch in the same place so that both long ends are on the right side. Unthread the needle and pull both ends to draw the stitched knot tight.

AGGEDOR

'The Curse of Peladon' brought us Aggedor, a sort of inter-galactic wild pig with very frightening tusks and claws, who turned out to be much nicer than he looks.

Make the basic puppet in any brown furry yarn in reversed st.st. to make him furrier still. With scraps of pink shiny yarn, in chain stitch, embroider a pink snout, with nostrils and an extra wrinkle line above, and two eyebrow lines. In black yarn in chain stitch, fill in the nostrils, add another wrinkle line and embroider eyes. In white yarn, place a tiny stitch in the eye to give expression. Make claws and tusks of white felt scraps and stitch on firmly.

ZYGON

'Terror of the Zygons' gave us Earth creatures all sorts of problems, Scotland's most famous legend included, when the Zygons were stranded at the bottom of Loch Ness. They are dirty, shiny greenish grey, and take their colour a great deal from the way the light falls on them.

Make the basic puppet in any metallic or shiny yarn. These yarns are often very fine, in which case knit together with another thin yarn. Fasten large beads open ends upwards, in lines down the Zygon's front below arm height, and down both sides of its head and upper arms to represent its suckers. Using a rough or tweedy mixture yarn, embroider single chain stitches in a random pattern across his shoulder line and middle, and around the beads to suggest the smaller suckers. Embroider in the same yarn a brow line and an angled line under the brow, leaving a space for the eye. Embroider the eyes in white in chain stitch, outline them in fine black yarn and add a small black spot in the eye to give expression. Add two small black stitches as nostrils between the eyes.

TIME LORDS IN ACTION*

Time Lords, of whom the Doctor is one, live for an immeasurable time, and appear in one regeneration after another. If you have an Action Man, you can create all the regenerations by dressing him, in turn, in these outfits, which convert him into whichever version of the Doctor you need for your game. There is even a pattern to turn him into another Time Lord, the Master, if you want a baddie. These costumes are fiddly to make, but using scraps they would be cheap to do, and would make a thoughtful, special, and spectacular present which would give hours of pleasure.

If you have several Action Men, you can choose blond or dark-haired ones appropriate to the different costumes, but only one is really neccessary as, after all, more than one version of the Doctor is rarely around at the same time, although you can of course use as many of your regenerated Doctor forms as you like in any games, plots and stories that you like. The Master has always been bearded and the beard here was made by teasing out tiny pieces of dark yarn and gluing them on. This can be very difficult to remove, so only do it if you want a permanently hirsute Action Man!

The basic patterns can also be adapted by using other colours for any other characters you would like, as the basic shirt and trousers are very simple and can be made from almost any material or yarn. All the versions of the Doctor have worn a traditional, costume-style jacket, often worn open. If you would like a modern jacket for a different character, add four stitches throughout to each front, then the fronts will meet and you will be able to fasten them with press studs or hooks. If adapting the pattern always remember to make the clothes generous, so that they are easier to put on.

Colour illustration is on page 2.

TO SEW THE BASIC SHIRT

One of these goes under the Doctors' costumes in white and for the Master in black. Cut out the shapes given (page 117) in felt and firmly oversew the shoulder seams and side seams, leaving a 1½in (4cm) deep armhole and letting the fronts simply overlap, before tucking into the trouser waist. They can be fastened with press studs if wished. Always sew very firmly and fasten on and off well, so that the garments will stand lots of tough play and taking on and off.

The shirts can be made of any other material instead, but, if using one that frays, cut out with a small seam allowance (about ¼in or 1cm) all round and hem all the edges after making shoulder and side seams.

TO KNIT THE BASIC TROUSERS

Use the following pattern in the colour and stitch pattern as given later for the particular costume that you want to make.

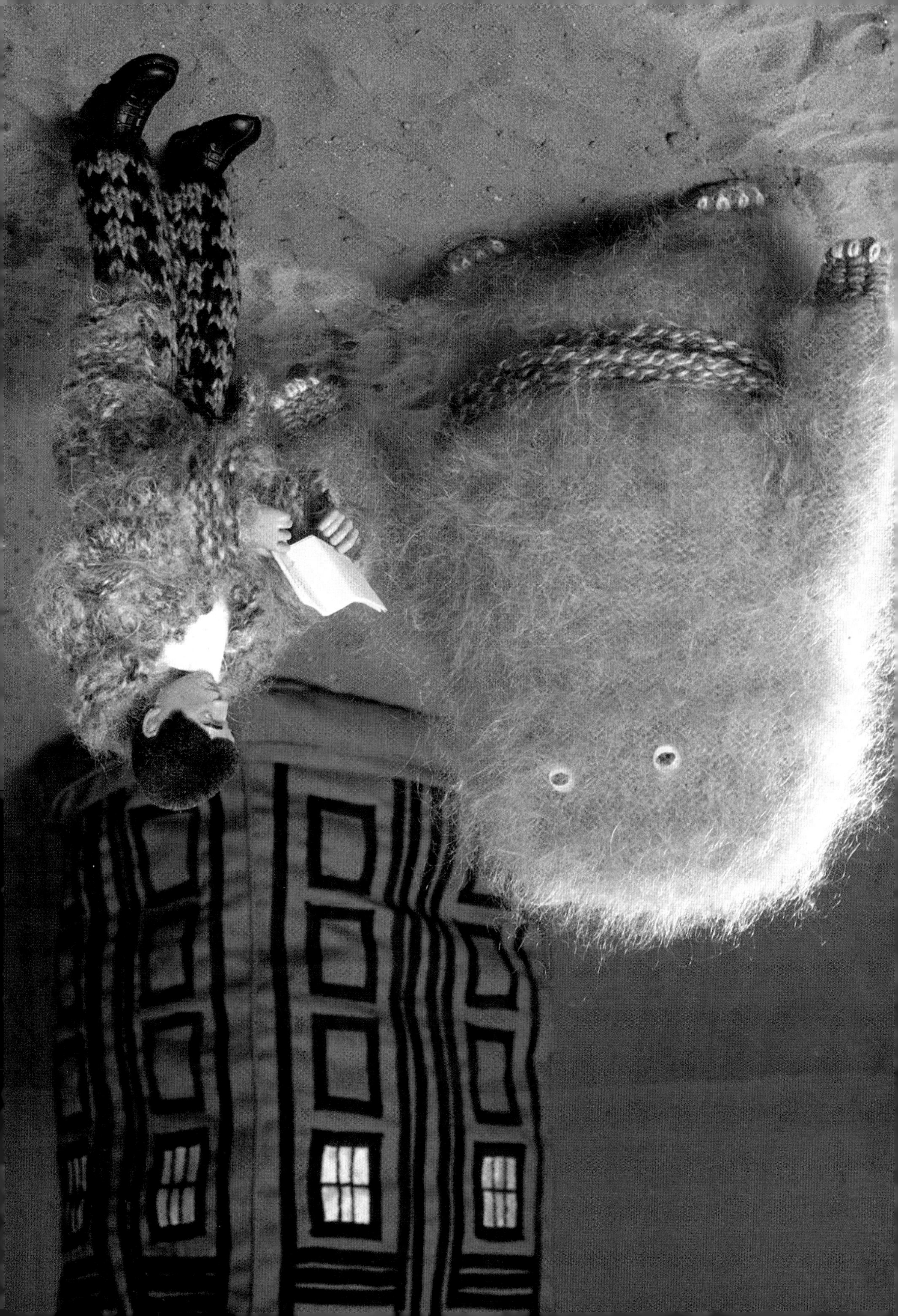

Materials
A small quantity of double knitting quality yarn in the chosen colour or colours; a small piece of millinery or fine elastic.

Tension
24 sts. and 32 rows = 4in (10cm) on size 8 (4mm, US size 5) needles in st.st.

Leg and body half
Make two, both alike.
Cast on 20 sts. Work 6in (15cm) straight in st.st. Cast off.

To make up
Fold each of the trouser pieces in half, lengthways, and seam 4½in (11½cm) from one end to within 1½in (3½cm) of the other end to form a tube 4½in (11½cm) long for the leg. Seam one remaining 1½in (3½cm) edge from one half of the trousers to one of the 1½in (3½cm) edges of the other half of the trousers, seaming together to form a join up the body front. Join the remaining two 1½in (3½cm) edges to form the back body seam. Thread the extreme top edge with the millinery or fine elastic and tie firmly, not too tight to get on, but sufficiently tightly to prevent his trousers from falling down!

TO KNIT THE BASIC JACKET
Use the following pattern in the colour as given later for the particular costume you want to make.

Materials
A small quantity of double knitting yarn in the chosen colour or colours. Trims and ribbons as given for the individual costumes.

Tension
24 sts. and 32 rows = 4in (10cm) on size 8 (4mm, US size 5) needles in st.st.

Back
Cast on 20 sts. K 2 rows. Cont. in st.st. starting K, until work measures 5in (12½cm). Cast off.

Right front
Cast on 5 sts. K 2 rows.
*Next row: K2, inc. 1 st. in next st., K to end.
Next row: P to last 2 sts., K2.
Repeat these two rows until there are 10 sts.
Keeping 2 sts. in K at right-hand edge, work straight in st.st. until front is 12 or 13 rows shorter than back, ending with a P row.
**Next row: K2, K2togtbl, K to end.

Next row: P to last 2 sts., K2.
Repeat these 2 rows until 6 sts. remain.
Work straight until front is same length as back. Cast off.

Left front
As for right front but reverse all shapings and edges, i.e. work shaping at * as follows:
K to last 3, inc. 1 st. in next st., K2.
Next row: K2, P to end.
Repeat these 2 rows until there are 10 sts.
Keep 2 sts. in K throughout on left-hand edge and work shaping at** as follow:
K to last 4, K2tog, K2.
Next row: K2, P to end.
Repeat these 2 rows until 6 sts. remain.

All shapings are thus reversed.

Sleeves
Make two, both alike.
Cast on 20 sts. and work 4in (10cm) straight in st.st.
Cast off.

To make up
Seam the sleeves into a tube. Join shoulder and side seams, inserting sleeves.

THE WILLIAM HARTNELL COSTUME
In black, brown and beige double knitting yarn and white felt.
Additional materials: scraps of narrow black ribbon.

To make
Work the trousers in beige and brown in the following checkered pattern:
Cast on in beige.
1st row: K, 1 st. beige, *1 st. brown, 3 sts. beige*, repeat from * to * to last 3, 1 st. brown, 2 sts. beige.
2nd row: P,* 3 sts. brown, 1 st. beige*, repeat from * to * to end.
3rd row: K,* 3 sts. brown, 1 st. beige*, repeat from * to * to end.
4th row: P, 1 st. beige,* 1 st. brown, 3 sts. beige*, repeat from * to * to last 3, 1 st. brown, 2 sts. beige.
Repeat these four rows.

Weave the spare yarn in as much as you can on the wrong side because his feet may catch in any large loops when the trousers are being put on.

Work the jacket in black. Make the shirt in white felt, turn the two collar corners onto the outside and catch down the corners to suggest a wing collar.

Make a bow with the scrap of black ribbon and stitch to the top of one shirt front.

THE PATRICK TROUGHTON COSTUME

In black and grey double knitting yarn, brown brushed yarn and white felt.
Additional materials: a short piece of string.

Work the trousers exactly as for William Hartnell but using grey instead of beige, and black instead of brown. The shirt is the basic one in white felt. Work the jacket in any thick, furry, pale brown mixture yarn to suggest the ragged fur coat, add 1½in (4cm) to the length of the back and fronts and work in rev.st.st.

Make the jacket collar as follows: cast on 16 sts. Work 5 rows. Cast off. Sew the collar centrally around the jacket neck opening.

Tie the waist with a piece of string.

THE JON PERTWEE COSTUME

In black and dark red double knitting yarn and white felt.
Additional materials: scraps of white and red satin ribbon; black yarn for cape.

Work the trousers in plain black and make the basic shirt in white felt. Run a gathering thread along the centre of a piece of white ribbon and gather to fit the distance from neck to waist. Sew down the centre front, attaching to one shirt front only, to make the dress-shirt frill. Make the jacket in dark red and embroider, in black, a deep cuff line, lapel lines, and frog fastenings, using stem stitch and chain stitches.

To make the cape

In black, cast on 60 sts. K 2 rows.
Work 5in (12½cm) in st.st., but keeping first and last 2 sts. in K throughout, ending with a P row.
Next row: K 15 sts. turn and work these sts. first.
*Next row: K2, P11, K2.
Next row: K.
Repeat these last 2 rows.
Work 1½in (4cm) in this way on these sts.
Cast off.*
Rejoin yarn and K centre 30 sts. and turn.
Next row: K2, P26, K2.
Next row: K.
Repeat these 2 rows.
Work until middle matches length of completed side.
Cast off.
Rejoin yarn to rem. 15 sts. and work as from * to *.

Fold the two cape fronts back vertically to the shoulder so that the fronts are double, then seam the shoulders through all three thicknesses. Catch this fold at the bottom edge, by seaming the doubled front together at the bottom too. Run a piece of red satin ribbon centrally down each front to suggest a satin lining.

THE TOM BAKER COSTUME

In dark brown and mid-brown double knitting yarn and white felt.
Additional materials: very small scraps of red, grey, dark brown, white and cream yarn for the scarf; scraps of brown felt; scraps of fine black ribbon.

Work the trousers in plain dark brown smooth or even shiny yarn, and the jacket in mid brown, adding 1½in (4cm) to the length of the back and fronts. Make a basic shirt in white felt.

To make the scarf, cast on 6 sts. and work in garter st. (every row K) changing colour at random to give stripes ranging from 2 rows to 10, in cream, white, grey, dark brown, pale brown and red in any order you like. Always make the colour change rows on the same side to give the scarf a wrong and a right side and join colours as carefully as possible to keep the scarf neat. Cast off when the scarf is about 26in (65cm) long. Stitch fringes along each end in a mixture of colours.

To make the hat, cut out a crown and brim from brown felt (see the pattern on page 117), also cut a strip 4½in × ⅜in (11½cm × 1cm). Stitch this strip into a ring, then stitch the bottom edge of this ring around the inside edge of the hole in the middle of the brim to form the hat sides. Easing the fullness of the sides in, stitch the top edge of this strip all around the crown. Trim with fine ribbon or yarn.

THE PETER DAVISON COSTUME

In cream and dark cream double knitting yarn and white felt.
Additional materials: red embroidery silk; scraps of very fine red ribbon and narrow red ribbon; scraps of white felt, tiny scrap of green felt.

Work the trousers in plain pale cream yarn, then embroider with back stitch in red embroidery silk, as many fine vertical stripes on them as you have patience for, (about ¼in [½cm] apart). Make a basic shirt in white felt and stitch narrow red ribbon all round the inside edge of the neck and down the top half of the inside edges of both fronts. Turn the two top corners of the shirt down onto the right side to show this ribbon, and catch down to form lapels. Work the jacket in dark cream, adding ½in (1½cm) to the length of the back and the fronts. Stitch a line of very fine ribbon around the edge of the whole jacket opening, about ⅜in (½cm) from the edge to suggest piping. Do the same around the cuff and also, in a short length, at each side to suggest a pocket top. These lines could be worked in back stitch as on the trousers or in couched red yarn if such fine ribbon cannot

be obtained. Cut a frilled leaf shape about 1in (2½cm) long from green felt and add a narrow stem of white felt about 1in (2½cm) long down the middle. Stitch to the lapel to form the famous stick of celery badge. To make the hat, use the same pattern and method as for Tom Baker's hat but use white felt, make the 4½in (11½cm) strip of felt ½in (1½cm) wide, and trim with narrow red ribbon. For a completely authentic look, acquire a pair of white boots or shoes or paint a black pair white using modelling paint.

THE COLIN BAKER COSTUME

Made in red and yellow double knitting yarn and white felt.
Additional materials: black double knitting yarn; scraps of yellow, blue tartan or checkered, and turquoise spotted ribbon, red and green enamel paint if desired.

Work the trousers in plain yellow and the jacket in plain red. Make the shirt in white felt. Embroider vertical stripes as an all-over pattern down the trousers in black double knitting yarn in back stitch, or any straight stitch. Tie a large floppy bow around the neck in spotted turquoise ribbon. Stitch a piece of tartan or checkered, mainly blue-coloured ribbon around the jacket neck to form lapels, and stitch yellow ribbon down the coat edges from the lapel ends to the bottom, to form revers. If you do not mind using up a pair of shoes for Colin Baker's regeneration of the Doctor, then, using enamel model paint, colour a spat shape in orange and the remainder of the upper in green on each shoe, leaving the edges of the sole black.

THE MASTER

In black double knitting and black felt.
Additional materials: small quantities of gold thread.

Make the basic shirt in black felt, and the basic trousers and jacket in plain black.

To make a collar:
In black yarn, cast on 13 sts.
Work 4 rows in st.st. beginning K row.
P 1 row.
Work 4 rows in st.st. beginning P row.
Cast off.
Fold in half along the ridge formed by the central purl row, stitch together and attach centrally around the neck edge of the jacket. Embroider with gold thread and chain stitch in a pattern of a wavy line and dots.

Chop and tease out a tiny amount of dark or black yarn as a beard and stick on in the distinctive Master style, but only do this if you want the beard to stay, as it may not come off. A beard could also be carefully drawn on, again indelibly, with the kind of felt-tipped pen that writes on plastic.

☆ ☆

The Yeti is an obvious choice for a cuddly toy, even if he is a baddie. Apparently, the first time the Yetis encountered the Doctor, they were so appealing that a conscious effort had to be made to make them more horrid. This one is so lovable he must be a baby – if you can have such a thing as a baby Yeti.

He is knitted in a mohair yarn which is extremely fluffy, but if you make him for a very young child it would be better to use a brushed double knitting yarn, because mohair tends to moult, if chewed! Yetis do not have eyes as such, but to give our Yeti character he has a pair of coloured toy cats' eyes, set sideways on, so that they look slightly evil rather than catty, and luminous to suggest the Yetis' dubious ability to zap people from the place where their eyes would be if they had any. Yetis also have evil tusks when they open their mouths, but this one has not teethed yet! Colour illustration is on page 76.

Measurements
The Yeti is about 12in (30cm) high.

Materials
5 × 25gm balls of mohair yarn or approximately 3 × 50gm balls of brushed double knitting yarn; about 500gm of washable toy stuffing; 1 pair of 12mm diameter luminous toy-cat safety-eyes; scraps of grey, cream, and brown-tweedy double knitting yarn.

Tension
24 sts. and 32 rows = 4in (10cm) on size 8 (4mm, US size 5) needles in reversed st.st. which is used throughout.

Main pieces
Make two, both alike.
Cast on 24 sts.
1st row: P.
2nd row: K, inc. 1 st. in every st. (48 sts.).
3rd row: P.
4th row: *K1, inc. 1 st. in next st. *, rep. from * to * to end (72 sts.).
Work straight to a total length of 5in (12½cm) ending with a P row.
Next row: (K2tog, K32, K2tog) twice.
Next row: P.
Next row: K
Next row: P.
Next row: (K2tog, K30, K2tog) twice.
Cont. in this way, losing 4 sts. on every 4th row to 44 sts.

Work straight to a total length of 13in (31½cm), ending with a P row.
*Next row: (K2tog) to end.
Next row: P*.
Repeat from * to *. (11 sts.)
Cast off.

Legs

Make two, both alike.
*Cast on 18 sts. and work 1in (2½cm) straight ending with a P row.
Next row: (K1, K2tog) repeat to end (12 sts.).
Next row: P*.

**Next row: (Inc. 1 st. in next st., K2◊, inc. 1 st. in next st.) 3 times.
Next row: P**.
Repeat from ** to ** adding 2 sts. to the number at ◊ each time, so adding 6 sts. on every 2nd row to 42 sts.

Work straight to a total length of 3in (7½cm).
Cast off.

Arms

Make two, both alike.
Work as for legs from * to *.
Next row: Inc. 1 st. in every st. (24 sts.)
Work 2in (5cm) straight.
Dec. 1 st. each end of every other row to 4 sts.
Cast off.

To make up

Brush all pieces on the reversed st.st. side to make them extra fluffy. Seam the two body halves together, matching cast-on and cast-off edges. Insert eyes with dark stripe horizontal, centrally, about 2½in (6½cm) below top seam, then stuff. Seam arms leaving top end open and stuff, without pushing the stuffing down into the hands, then attach open-ended to the shoulders. Seam legs leaving top end open, and stuff without pushing the stuffing down into the feet, then attach open-ended to the base.

Without cutting the yarn, carefully trim the fluff from the hands and feet. Using grey, double knitting, stitch horizontal lines of straight stitch on both sides through the hands and feet to suggest the fingers and toes. Add claws in cream with single chain stitches. Make a long twisted cord or plait in tweed yarn and wind several times round the middle below the arms, for the girdle. If the toy is for an older child this could be tucked in or tied and therefore removeable, but for a baby it should be firmly stitched on.

CELERY BROOCH*

Peter Davison's costume for the Doctor seems incomplete without his stick of celery, so, for fun, you may like to make this one for yourself. There are various ways of doing it. You could use a real celery, but that causes problems. It dies for instance, you get greenfly instead of dandruff, and persuading a pin to stay in a celery stem is an excellent way of wasting an afternoon. People might even eat it! You could go for beautiful pottery, or composition, or moulded models, but few of us have the skill. So here is a pattern to make a celery brooch from scraps of felt, which is much easier, lighter to wear, and infinitely less edible.

Sewing pattern is on page 111.

Materials
Scraps of white felt, and scraps of felt in a variety of pale greens; yellow cotton or embroidery thread; safety-pin; very small quantity of stuffing or cotton wool.

Measurements
The brooch is about 7in (18cm) long and 4in (10cm) wide at its widest point.

To make
1. Using the pattern drawing, cut two stem shapes from white felt and six leaf shapes from felts in an assortment of greens.

2. Place the two stem shapes together so that they match and oversew them together, then lightly stuff the main stem with a very thin layer of teased stuffing.

3. Using yellow thread, work lines of back stitch up the stem, taking the needle through both layers of felt and any stuffing. The lines are parallel up the stem about ⅛in (½cm) apart, then travel up the 'branches' to their ends. This represents the ridges on the celery, and also gives the felt extra thickness and support.

4. Arrange the six leaves as you wish on the branches, and run a line of back stitch down each leaf centre, using the stitches to attach the leaf to the branch where the two overlap. It is easiest to begin with the underneath leaf or leaves first. You can of course have as many or as few leaves as you wish, and vary the colours according to the materials available, but do not get too carried away if you wish the brooch to look like the real one.

5. Firmly stitch a safety-pin onto the back of the stem.

K·9

K9 SHOULDER BAG ☆☆

K9 has always been a helpful and useful companion. What better way to keep him by your side could there be, than to turn him into a shoulder bag? (He has a shape that has always been reminiscent of a handbag anyway, but don't tell him, I don't think he would like it!) This bag can be made of any strong but still stitchable fabric, which could be waterproof or not, but which does need to be flexible, either grey or silver, If you use a washable material, it is logical for all the trim to be washable too, so use ribbon or embroidery instead of felt for the lettering and the tracking sensors (ears). Sewing pattern is on pages 110–11.

Materials

¾yd (¾m) of main fabric, 45in (114cm) wide; 7½in (19cm) of Velcro or similar hook-and-loop fastening, or press-studs if preferred; scraps of white felt and narrow dark red ribbon; three small pale beads; two shiny silver buttons; small quantity of safe and, if necessary, washable stuffing; about 6in (15cm) of red tartan ribbon; scrap of silver thread; dog tag or equivalent (for example, a small disc of card painted silver on both sides with a hole pierced through it).

Measurements

The bag base is approximately 9½in × 5½in (24cm × 14cm) and the bag is 6½in (16½cm) high, excluding the head.

To make

1. Using the pattern drawings, cut two head pieces, one the reverse of the other, one of each head gusset piece, one base, one side piece, two end pieces, one main side and top piece, and a strip 3in × 28in (7½cm × 71cm), or desired length, for the strap.

2. Across the stitching lines shown on the drawing on the main piece and ends, stitch a very small surface tuck on the right side.

3. With right sides together seam the two ends into the main piece, matching the two top tucks on the main piece to the two top corners of each end, and matching the third tuck all round the middle of the sides. Seam from the bottom of the sides to the third tuck *only* i.e. seaming the sides and top, leaving the untucked flap free.

4. With right sides together seam the remaining side piece between the ends, matching the ends of its bottom raw edge to the bottom raw edges of the other pieces.

5. With right sides together, seam in the base, matching all corners.

6. Neaten all the raw edges of the opening of the bag.

7. Attach the Velcro strip to close the bag (or use press-studs if you prefer).

8. Cut the K9 lettering out of white felt (use the knitting chart on page 69 as a guide if you wish) and stick or sew this centrally to the bag flap.

9. Double the strap strip right side out, and turn the raw edges in. Stitch along both long edges to make the strap and very firmly attach the strap ends to each side of the bag, centrally, at the top of the side piece, turning all raw edges under.

10. With right sides together join the two narrower ends of the head gussets.

11. With right sides together, insert this joined gusset between the two matching head pieces, placing the join at the top point of the nose. Seam in but do not close the gussets together. Stuff through this opening.

12. Attach the head to the bottom 2½in (6½cm) of the front of the strap and the first 1in (2½cm) of the side piece, neatening all raw edges and placing the head centrally.

13. Cut four 1in (2½cm) wide ovals of white felt and stitch together in pairs, gathering along one long edge. Stitch on through a bead, on top of the head as the tracking sensor 'ears'.

14. Stitch three strips of red ribbon across the front of the head gusset at eye height to form the visual orientation circuits, and centrally stitch on a silver button with a bead in the middle of these as the retractable data-com probe. Stitch the remaining button centrally on the nose as the photon blaster.

15. If you prefer, you can cut a rectangle of card to fit into the bottom of the bag to help to keep the shape.

16. Stitch a ring of the tartan ribbon to lie around the neck and tie the dog-tag or silver card loosely to it with the silver thread.

TARDIS SLEEPING BAG/QUILT ☆☆

If you sleep in or under a TARDIS you might wake up any time! This very simple version of the TARDIS has all you need, even doors that open in the middle, just like the real thing. It can be used as a bed cover, in which case it is opened flat and reaches from the bottom of the bed to pillow height, making the bed look like a TARDIS. Or it can be closed up the middle, making a generous sleeping bag 54in (137cm) long. This TARDIS is made from ready-made quilting, although you can if you wish make your own from a double layer of fine material with quilting wadding in between. It is much easier to stitch the window and door panel outlines to this kind of home-made wadding if it is previously caught together with a regular pattern of self colour lines of stitching, it can then be treated in just the same way as bought quilting. It is a good idea to ensure that all constituent materials are washable. It is also easy to add to the length of the TARDIS quilt by simply cutting all three pieces longer than 54in (137cm) to whatever length you like, and leaving a plain area of blue above and below the pattern of lines and windows.

If you prefer, the sleeping bag alternative could also be fastened with two 16in (41cm) open-ended zips at the bottom and a 54in (137cm) zip up the centre, or it could be folded in half and zipped in the conventional way along the bottom and up one side. This second way, however, looses the fun of the TARDIS doors opening properly down the middle.

Colour illustration is on page 29.

Materials
One piece of blue quilted material 33in × 55in (84cm × 140cm) and two pieces each 17½in × 55in (44cm × 140cm), or longer if required; 86in (218cm) of 1in (2½cm) wide Velcro, or similar press-strip-fastening (this is needed only for the sleeping bag alternative); 48 yd (43m) of ½in (1½cm) wide black tape or ribbon (if this is difficult to obtain or too expensive, one ball of any thick knitting yarn in black could be substituted); four 7in × 11in (18cm × 28cm) rectangles of any grey or silver washable fabric.

Measurements
The bed cover is 54in × 65in (137cm × 165cm), which folds into a sleeping bag 54in × 32in (137cm × 81cm).

To make
1. Make the two side seams by placing the two front pieces on the back piece, right sides together, and stitching a ½in (1cm) seam up the whole of each side.

2. Neaten by turning and stitching under a ½in (1cm) turning around the whole edge.

3. Stitch on the black tape or ribbon in the pattern that follows, neatening all ends, or couch down the black yarn in the same pattern, that is, stitch it down firmly along the given lines.

Special note: In the pattern lines described in this section, the measurements are taken throughout from the *centre* of one tape to the *centre* of the next, not, from one edge to another. This centre line would also be the one on which the black yarn, if substituted, would be couched down.

(a) With right side facing find the centre back of the sleeping bag, between the two seams and therefore approximately 16in (41cm) from each seam. Stitch two black lines the complete length of the back, each ¾in (2cm) away from this centre line, one on either side of it.
(b) Stitch two further parallel lines outside these two lines, and 1in (2½cm) away from them on either side, again the full length of the back.
(c) Stitch two more parallel lines the full length of the back, the first 1¾in (4½cm) away from one side seam, and the second 1in (2½cm) away from the first.
(d) Repeat as for the last two lines, but down the other side.
(e) In the two large spaces left between these three sets of parallel lines, place and stitch three parallel lines going across, the first 2¼in (6cm) from the top edge, the following two at 1in (2½cm) intervals below them.

4. In the two areas left between the black lines and the bottom edge, evenly arrange and mark out with pins eight rectangles, four in each area. Each rectangle is 11in (28cm) high and 7in (18cm) wide, and they should be arranged so that the spaces between one rectangle and another, and between them and the lines, are equal, and match. The rectangles at the bottom edge should be 1in (2½cm) away from this edge.

5. Pin or tack two of the grey/silver pieces of fabric onto the top two marked rectangles.

6. In the same way as described in 3 above, stitch one black line horizontally across the centre of each silver rectangle, and two vertical lines in black spaced centrally 2¼in (6cm) apart. All three of these lines should reach only to the edges of each silver rectangle.

7. Stitch a black line all around the silver rectangles; if in tape, so that its outside edge just covers the raw edges of the silver fabric; if in yarn, stitch down actually on the raw edges.

8. Repeat the shape of the top rectangles on the six marked rectangles below in stitched black lines as before. There is no silver fabric, nor are there any additional lines in these six rectangles.

9. Repeat the pattern exactly as given for half of the back on each front, ensuring that the black line nearest the opening edge is at least 1¼in (3cm) away from the edge. If the TARDIS is to be used as a bedspread it is now finished.

10. To convert the bedspread into a sleeping bag, or to make it useable as either, attach one side of a 54in (137cm) strip of Velcro to the inside of one opening edge, on the edge, and attach the other side of the same Velcro strip to match it on the outside of the other opening edge, on the edge.

11. Attach one side of the remaining 32in (81cm) of Velcro strip across the inside of the bottom edge of the back of the sleeping bag. Cut the other side of the Velcro into two halves each 16in (41cm) long and attach these, to match, one inside the bottom edge of each front, so that the TARDIS closes centrally.

TARDIS TIDY ☆ ☆

The idea of a tidy TARDIS seems a contradiction in terms. The real thing is certainly not very tidy in its habits! On the other hand the inside of the TARDIS does seem to contain everything, so there is an excuse, if you need one, for making this door-hanging covered in pockets which hold a surprising amount of bits and bobs, toys and Whovian ephemera, hankies and things that would go up the Hoover, *Doctor Who* comics and hair grips. It is designed to hang from a hook on the back of a door, but you can, of course, hang it from any wall or piece of furniture that you wish, bearing in mind that it is about 5 feet (152cm) high, and narrow enough to clear the knob on an ordinary door. An ideal material would be denim. Any strong material would do of course, but denim, as well as being strong, has exactly the faded blue colour of the early 1960s Metropolitan police telephone box in which form the TARDIS has remained, by mistake, since its chameleon circuit failed on a visit to Earth at that time. Many of the Doctor's adventures have been enlivened by problems with the TARDIS, but your untidiness problems at least should be solved by this version.

Colour illustration is on page 64, sewing pattern page 112.

Materials

2¼yd (2m) of blue denim or similar strong material 36in (90cm) wide; two rectangles of silver or grey material 7in × 8½in (18cm × 21½cm); 19yd (17m) of ½in (1cm) wide black tape or ribbon (if this is difficult to obtain or too expensive one ball of any thick knitting yarn in black could be substituted, but even if you do use yarn, ½yd (45cm) of any ½in (1cm) wide tape is still needed as well); a wire coat hanger.

Measurements

The total length is approximately 5 feet (152cm) including the hanger hook. Width at widest point is 23½in (60cm), the width of the main part is 22in (56cm).

To make

1. Cut out one main piece in denim, using the pattern drawing for the top and base as given, and extending the side lines so that, between the top and the base, the edge measurement is 45in (114cm). Cut out eight denim rectangles and two silver grey fabric rectangles from the given pattern.

2. Turn the seam allowance onto the wrong side all around the main piece and stitch down.

3. The placing lines on the pattern drawing represent the position of the centre line of the tape, or the stitching line for the black yarn. Using these lines as a

guide, stitch down the tape onto the main piece, neatening all ends, or couch down the black yarn by stitching it on, in the pattern of lines as shown, excluding pocket lines.

4. Turn the seam allowance on to the wrong side around all edges of each denim pocket rectangle and tack or pin into place.

5. Turn the seam allowance onto the wrong side around all edges of the silver/grey rectangles, and tack or pin them into position over two of the denim rectangles, matching the pocket shape with the denim rectangle.

6. On these two silver/grey rectangles *only,* stitch on, in the same way as for the main piece, the grid of black lines across the rectangles, as shown on the pattern drawing.

7. On all eight rectangles – two silver/grey and six denim – pin or tack into position a black line around the complete edge, at the edge. Stitch this line down along one short edge only, so hemming the edge and catching down all trim and hems. This short edge now becomes the top.

8. Place the silver/grey rectangles, top edge up, and right side out, as shown on the pattern, to make the TARDIS windows. Space the remaining six rectangles evenly, three per side, in the remaining area, to make the panels in the TARDIS, leaving equal spaces between them. Ensure that the top edge is towards the top, and they are right sides out. Pin or tack into place.

9. Stitch each rectangle down on both its long sides and across the bottom, catching down all trim, black lines and hems, so forming each rectangle into a pocket.

10. Place the wire coat hanger on the back of the TARDIS so that its long bottom wire lies centrally across the work behind the position of the second black line from the top. Cover this bottom wire with a line of tape and stitch firmly into place. Put a small piece of tape over the neck of the hanger, i.e. the straight bottom half of the hook and stitch firmly into place, so securing the hanger to the back of the work.

CONSOLE FLOOR CUSHION ☆☆

The control console is the very heart of the TARDIS. From it all the mind-boggling functions of the time-machine are originated; the guidance systems, the drive systems, the environmental control and all the navigation. These functions are powered by a wonderfully complicated collection of read-out screens, displays, controls, visual display units, mechanisms and computers. Imagination can run riot with ideas, dreams and games based on the things which such technical wizardry would allow one to do.

This floor cushion takes the basic hexagon of the console, makes it squashy enough to sit, lie or fall on. It is then covered with buttons to press, screens to gaze at, grills to speak into and levers to push, so that you can simply sit on it in a fairly dignified way, or if you are young enough, either in years or at heart, you can have endless fun with the adventures that pressing some of those buttons will lead you to, and rescue you from.

The console is pale in colour, a problem with a floor cushion, so you need to decide whether to make all the trimming washable, or whether you will be dry-cleaning the cover. You could if you have the patience, take all the trim off every time you wash or clean it. It is worth thinking of this aspect before choosing your trimmings, and before choosing the basic fabric, which will also need to be cleaned periodically.

The whole cushion is far too big to wash complete, unless you have a very unconventional gigantic washing machine, or equally unconventional gigantic muscles! So washability is not a consideration when choosing the stuffing, but, because of the quantity, you will need to consider not just price, but weight. Fire retardant polystyrene beads, acrylic toy or quilt stuffing, or even the contents of an old eiderdown or a couple of old pillows would be fine.

If you wish you could make or buy piping cord and insert this in all the seams of the outer cover to give a ridge all along the outer edges.

Colour illustration is on page 73, sewing pattern page 113.

Materials

2yd (1.75m) of lining fabric in a pale colour and 2 yd (1.75m) of outer fabric in cream or grey, both 45in (114cm) wide; scraps of fabric, ribbon and tape; exciting, hi-tech-looking buttons, beads or anything you fancy to create the details (see instruction 9 below), suitable stuffing.

Measurements

The console cushion is about 26in (65cm) across and about 10in (25cm) high.

To make

The lining and the outer cover are made in exactly the same way, and all

instructions 1–5 below are repeated with the two different fabrics.

1. Cut out one hexagonal base, one hexagonal top, six edge pieces and six shaped surface side pieces.

2. With right sides together, join the side seams of the six shaped surface pieces each one to the next, so creating a hexagon with a hole in the centre.

3. With right sides together, seam the smaller hexagonal top piece into the hole in the centre of the top, matching each corner to a seam.

4. With right sides together, seam the short sides of the rectangular edge pieces together, each one to the next, then the last to the first again, so forming them into the vertical wall of the edge.

5. With right sides together, seam the large hexagonal cushion top into the sides matching each seamed corner of the top with a seamed corner of the sides.

6. With right sides together, seam in the large hexagonal base, again matching each of its corners with the seamed corners of the sides. In the lining, leave one long base side seam open, in the cover leave open two long base sides together.

7. Stuff the lining and close the remaining seam.

8. Neaten around the raw edges of the opening left on the cover.

9. Leaving the hexagonal top and base, and vertical sides plain, decorate each of the six shaped faces as a side of the console. You can really use your imagination and do your own thing, but some of the things used here are screens made of squares or concentric circles of fabric, some framed in ribbon; rings of fabric; shiny metallic or brightly coloured buttons arranged in groups or rows; button 'knobs' on ribbon 'levers', groups or rows of coloured beads; beads or buttons as on/off switches; rows of ribbon or tape arranged as grills; and pieces of metallic yarn or ribbon used to define areas such as the hexagonal top. Most of these decorations will all be more satisfactory if stitched on, although flat fabric pieces can be glued. Do bear in mind that safety must be a consideration when choosing these decorations and attaching them, especially if the user is very young.

10. Put the cover over the lining cushion and close the opening in some way which can easily be re-opened to remove the cover for cleaning, for example, hand-stitching, press-studs, or even a zip-fastener.

TARDIS CUSHION ☆☆

Maybe you will be able to use this cushion, rather like a legendary magic carpet, to fly anywhere in the universe, in any time zone. Maybe! Even if it does not have quite such spectacular powers, it is certainly fun to play with, and practical and comfortable to use. So why not make your own TARDIS?

This TARDIS took about 3kg of washable toy stuffing, but you could use fire retardant polystyrene beads, or chopped foam, or any safe stuffing material you like. If the cushion is for a small child, be especially sure that the stuffing is non-toxic, washable and not too heavy. This TARDIS is ideal for carrying around and sitting on in front of the television to watch the latest episode of *Doctor Who,* but little ones will stagger under the weight of it, or you will have to carry it around for them all the time, if it is too heavy.

Like the other two versions of the TARDIS in this book, the black lines here are made with stitched-on tape. If you prefer, stitch down a thick black yarn instead, as this would almost certainly be cheaper.

Colour illustration is on page 85, sewing pattern page 114.

Materials

1yd (1m) of blue denim, or similar strong material 45in (114cm) wide; 28yd (25¼m) of ⅜in (1cm) wide black ribbon or tape, or a ball of chunky thick black yarn; scraps of silvery grey material, scraps of thin black yarn; about 3kg of washable toy stuffing, or equivalent.

Measurements

The cushion is about 20in (50cm) high and 11in (28cm) across.

To make

1. Cut out four side pieces, one rooftop piece, four step top pieces and four step side pieces from the denim material. Also cut one square base with sides the same length as the long sides of the rectangular side of step piece.

2. In silver grey material, cut eight rectangles each 2in × 2½in (5cm × 6½cm) and pin two of these on each side piece in the position shown for the two top windows.

3. Decorate each side piece with lines of tape or with stitched-down black yarn, in the design shown in the pattern drawing, neatening the edges of the rectangles of silver grey material under the black lines which form the edges of the two top windows.

4. Couch, or stitch down the finer black yarn over the silver grey material to form the window frame pattern, in the positions shown on the pattern drawing.

5. With right sides together, seam the four side pieces together, along their long sides to form the main box shape and roof.

6. Stitch the square rooftop piece into the hole which results where the tops of the roof sides form a square.

7. With right sides together, stitch each step side piece to a step top piece along its longer edge, then, with right sides together, stitch the ends of these double pieces together to form the complete square of steps. The seams which form the sharp outer corner of the step can also be top stitched around the outside on the right side to give the step better definition if desired.

8. With right sides together, seam the step onto the main part of the TARDIS, matching all corner seams.

9. With right sides together, seam in the base along three sides only, matching the corners to the corner seams.

10. Stuff as firmly as you wish, and close the remaining seam.

K9 CUSHION ☆☆

K9 makes a terrific cushion, a lovely rounded comfy version of the animated tin box we all know and love.

It is a good idea to make him out of a fairly firm fabric so that he keeps his shape well. If you will want to wash him, make a separate inner cover for the body only and stuff the head with washable stuffing. Then make the body cover removeable from the inner body cushion by loosely slip stitching a long base seam or fitting a zip. If you do this, remember to make all the trimmings washable too – substitute scraps of washable material for the felt and make his dog-tag removeable. He would also be rather splendid in PVC or similar waterproof material, especially if it is shiny or metallic, and he would then wipe clean too. Be sure that your sewing machine or your fingers have the strength and stamina to cope with sewing such a thick fabric.

Colour illustration is on pages 74–5, sewing pattern on page 115.

Materials

1¼yd (1.2m) of strong grey or silvery fabric, 45in (114cm) wide; scraps of felt or similar fabric in white; scraps of red ribbon; about ½yd (40cm) of red tartan ribbon; scraps of strong silver thread; circular dog-tag (or a pierced circle cut from silver painted card); 2 large buttons, one bright domed button and one metal button; 9 medium-sized matching coloured buttons; suitable stuffing, washable if required, and an optional 15in (37cm) zip-fastener or press-fasteners.

To make

1. Cut out two ends, two sides, one base, one top, one of each head gusset and two head pieces one the reverse of the other.

2. Across the lower stitching lines on each of the sides and each of the ends, stitch as small as possible a tuck, onto the right side.

3. Stitch similar tucks, on the same four main pieces, on the upper stitching line, but stitch this tuck all across onto the wrong side.

4. With right sides together, stitch the end pieces to the side pieces, matching all tuck lines and corners.

5. With right sides together, insert the top, stitching it in all around its four sides and matching each of its corners to each of the corner seams of the body.

6. With right sides together, insert the base, stitching it in around both short sides and one long side and matching each of its corners to each of the corner

seams of the body. (If you wish to make a lining, cut two ends, two sides, a base and the top in lining fabric and repeat 2–6 above with these lining pieces.)

7. If you have made a lining cushion, firmly stuff it through the open long base edge and stitch this final seam closed. Then place this cushion inside the outer cover and slip stitch the remaining seam closed in a way that can be easily undone for removal and washing, or, if you wish, insert a zip in this final top cover seam, or close it with press-fasteners. If you are not lining the cushion, stuff the body section and neatly and permanently close the final seam.

8. With right sides together, seam together the two short ends of the head gussets.

9. Matching this seam to the point of the nose, and with right sides together, seam the long sides of the top head gusset along the top edges of the two head pieces, and the long sides of the bottom head gusset along the bottom edges of the two head pieces.

10. Stuff the head and close the remaining seam between the two gusset ends.

11. Stitch three parallel pieces of red ribbon across the head at eye level, and stitch a large button with a metal button in the middle of it, centrally between the bottom and second of these ribbon strips. Stitch the other large button, with the domed button in the middle of it, centrally at the top of the front of the nose.

12. Cut four 2in (5cm) wide ovals of white felt or fabric scraps and stitch them together in pairs to make ears. Gather one long bottom edge of each ear and stitch by this edge onto the top of the front of the head, arranging the pair of ears evenly.

13. Firmly stitch the head onto the top of the front of the cushion or its outer cover.

14. Stitch the red tartan ribbon around the neck as a collar, and from it, using the silver thread, hang the dog-tag or disc of silver card.

15. Stitch on the remaining buttons in a pattern on the back to suggest the buttons which operate K9.

16. Cut out, from white felt, 'K9' in suitable computer style lettering about 3in (7½cm) high, and stick them on K9's right-hand side, centrally, in the upper half, with a spot between them (use the charts on page 69 for the K9 lettering on the knitted version as a guide if you wish).

SEW A NASTY ☆

Here are more of the delicious *Doctor Who* baddies. These are sewn and are very simple to make. A fabric glove puppet is one of the most basic toy ideas, and they are so satisfying to use that I defy anyone with any scrap of childhood left in them to put one on without animating it a little, making it wave or pull a face. The pattern that follows is only a basic guide to making your puppets. Your imagination and the use of available materials can do the rest. Sometimes the materials suggest the creature, sometimes you need to rummage in your rag-bag for appropriate bits. If you or your family are puppet addicts, you should collect remnants, felt and other scraps, bits of ribbon and lace, and never throw the horridest buttons away – one day they will give some puppet or other just the expression you need. Colour illustration is on pages 30–1.

The pattern drawing for the puppets (page 116) gives the basic shape and fits the average hand. To be sure it will fit you, measure around the widest part of your hand (about at the thumb base) and add about 2in (5cm). Half of this measurement is the puppet's width. If your character requires it, it can, of course be as wide as you like, but do not try to give a glove puppet a tight waist or he will be difficult to get on, although he can have a skirt which sticks out below where his waist would be if he had one!

Puppets can be as long as you like. If they are too short they become difficult to operate, as the audience keeps catching sight of bits of wrist. But there is no restriction on length and they can cover the whole arm, if you wish, and if it suits the character – the Loch Ness Monster perhaps?

The puppets are easier to operate if their arms are attached at an angle, if they have arms at all, and these should be fairly generous. If the arms are much longer than those given here, they may flop, which may be what you want, or you could strengthen the extended arm with an adhesive-taped roll of thin card inside. Exceptionally long arms can be operated by a second puppeteer if they are attached to rods.

TO MAKE THE BASIC PUPPET

Materials

Two pieces of material about 8in × 5in (20cm × 12½cm), or as required. Scraps of materials for arms, and additional trim, scraps for decoration.

Measurements

Each puppet to this basic pattern is about 8in (20cm) high and 5in (12½cm) wide, but this can of course, be varied as much as you like.

To make

1. Cut two body pieces, and four arm pieces, two the reverse of the other two, in the main fabric.

2. Stitch the arm pieces together in pairs, leaving the straight end open, with whichever kind of sewing stitch suits the material best, by hand or machine.

3. Stitch the two body pieces together in the same way, inserting the arms at an upward angle about half-way up the puppet or at the height comfortable for the puppeteer.

4. Decorate according to instructions given below, or in any way you wish, to create your chosen character.

SEA DEVIL

These reptilian marine creatures, alone or in cahoots with the equally scaly Silurians, seem determined to take over the Earth, which should make for some exciting puppet plays.

Make the basic puppet in any grey fabric, then stitch on a patch of brown fabric trimmed to the distinctive beaked face-shape of the Sea Devil. Stitch on button eyes with central brown spots of felt stuck on to give expression. Embroider a fierce frown between the eyes and also the beak shape of the mouth, the nostrils and the shocking bags under his eyes! Stitch together a very simple-shaped baggy shirt for him made of netting (a scrap of old curtain perhaps, or a netting duster or dish cloth?). Stitch onto his right hand an exterminating gun, i.e. a flat white button with a line around it and a central dot painted on. To get the scribbled effect on the net shirt, do just that – scribble on it! Use paint or a felt-tipped pen, and to stop the colour going everywhere put some paper under until it is dry.

MANDRELL

Like many *Doctor Who* baddies, the Mandrells have a certain charm in spite of their distinctly anti-social behaviour, and although they are part of a 'Nightmare in Eden' they are appealing enough to make a delightful puppet.

Make the basic puppet in any orangey/red material, then cover him in scales all over except the head. This can be done by drawing in felt-tipped pen or paint, or stitching on wavy-edged ribbon all over in overlapping strips, or – if you have the patience, and the result would certainly be most spectacular – cover him in sequins. These can be purchased in strip or sheet form, to cut down on some of the work. Or you could cover him in overlapping strips of felt with a wavy bottom edge. Over the head, stitch two pieces of dark fur fabric cut to the shape of the head top, with the front piece about 2½in (6½cm) deep, the back piece 4in (10cm) deep. Stitch narrow strips of the same fabric around the wrists. Embroider claws with white yarn. Cut, in green felt and about 1¾in (4½cm) across, the chracteristic scallop or clam-shaped face piece, and stitch it down on top of the front fur fabric piece. Stitch dark green shiny buttons either side of this as eyes. From the green face-shape stitch on, and allow to hang down, four or five lengths of pale brown yarn about 2–3in (5–7½cm) long to make the mouth tentacles.

CYBERMATS*

When an overambitious team of archaeologists decided to excavate the Tomb of the Cybermen, they released a flurry of metallic woodlice called Cybermats, which, despite their rather charming appearance, have very nasty habits which can have fatal consequences for their enemies. But they do make very satisfying toys, if only because of their holdable shape, and they would also fit in rather well with a puppet show or play. You can, if you wish, scale the basic pattern (page 116) down and make tiny Cybermats, to use with the Action Men versions of the Doctor. If you make Cybermats for a very young fan, use circles of felt for the eyes and tufts of wool for the antennae, for safety's sake.

Materials
Pieces of grey felt or any other non-fray grey or silver material. Each Cybermat takes two pieces, one about 10in × 3in (25cm × 7½cm), the other about 10in × 5in (25cm × 12½cm), plus some scraps: two silver domed buttons and about 16 very small beads of assorted shapes and colours; tiny scraps of black felt; a small quantity of safe toy stuffing.

Measurements
The Cybermat is about 9in (23cm) long and about 2in (5cm) high.

To make
1. Cut one top piece and one base piece from the fabric, using the pattern drawing. Also cut one rectangular piece 1in × 3in (2½cm × 7½cm) and two rectangular pieces 1in × 2in (2½cm × 5cm). Cut a rough fringe in these three strips about ½in (1cm) deep along one long edge. These pieces will form the fringes of whiskers round the front of the Cybermat.

2. Stitch together all the darts in the top piece by oversewing.

3. Pin or tack the whisker strips with their long uncut edges ¼in (½cm) under the edges of the top piece, with the longest strip centrally at the round end (the front) and the two shorter pieces at the sides, beginning ½in (1cm) away from the ends of the front piece.

4. Stitch in the base, matching the bottom and top shapes, and stitching in the whisker strips between the two main pieces as you come to them. Stuff the Cybermat before finally closing this seam.

5. Stitch on the eye buttons, or circles of white felt with a tiny circle of black felt glued on to give the distinctive eye centre.

6. Make antennae by threading a small quantity of very small beads, with a larger bead top and bottom. If these are stitched on with the thread which runs through them pulled very tight, they will stand up. Or make tassels of wool and attach.

DOCTOR
WHO

SEWING PATTERNS

HOW TO USE THE SEWING PATTERNS

The sewing patterns are drawn to various scales given under the headings for each pattern. A few are given as actual size. In these cases, simply trace off the pattern, place the shape on the fabric, and cut. Where the patterns need enlarging (i.e. where the scale is given as 1cm = 2in, or 1cm = 1in.):

1. Trace the pattern onto 1cm squared graph paper.
2. Use this graph tracing as a guide to mark the main points of the pattern on 1in or 2in squared graph paper (depending on the scale given) by counting the squares between one point and another.
3. Join up the points with straight lines or curves as on the original pattern to produce an enlarged version of the pattern.
4. Place the enlarged pattern on the fabric and cut.

Remember that an unbroken line represents a cutting line, except where it states PLACE ON FOLD. An allowance of ½in (1½cm) has been made throughout for hems and seams except where otherwise stated. Stitching lines are marked with a row of regular short dashes. For two of the patterns (Tegan's Boob Tube and Romana's Sailor Top) 3 sizes are given with alternative cutting lines. Make sure you are following the cutting line you require. The arrows on the patterns indicate which way the grain of the fabric should go.

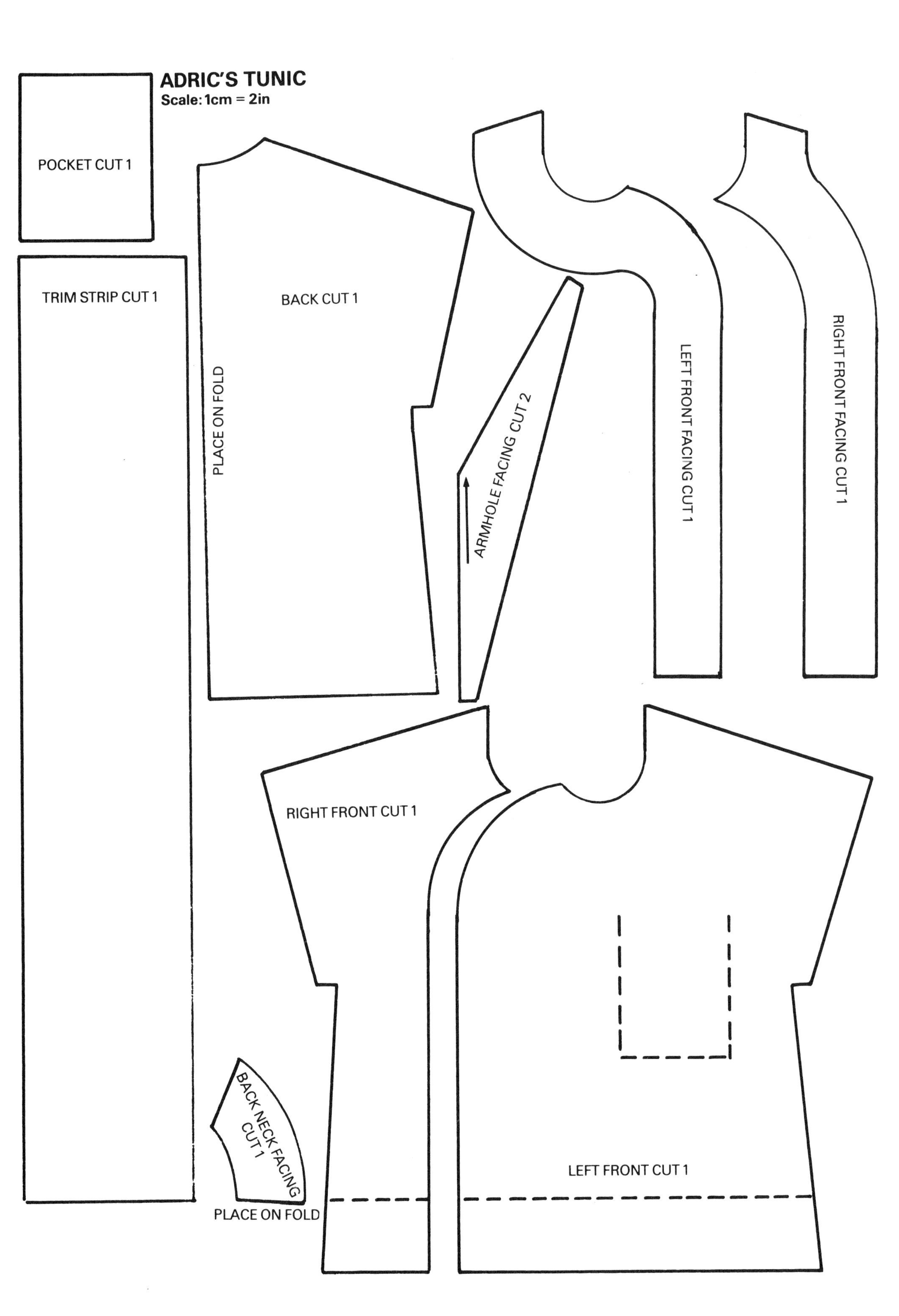
ADRIC'S TUNIC
Scale: 1cm = 2in
POCKET CUT 1
TRIM STRIP CUT 1
BACK CUT 1
PLACE ON FOLD
ARMHOLE FACING CUT 2
LEFT FRONT FACING CUT 1
RIGHT FRONT FACING CUT 1
RIGHT FRONT CUT 1
BACK NECK FACING
CUT 1
PLACE ON FOLD
LEFT FRONT CUT 1

ROMANA'S SAILOR TOP

Scale: 1cm = 2in

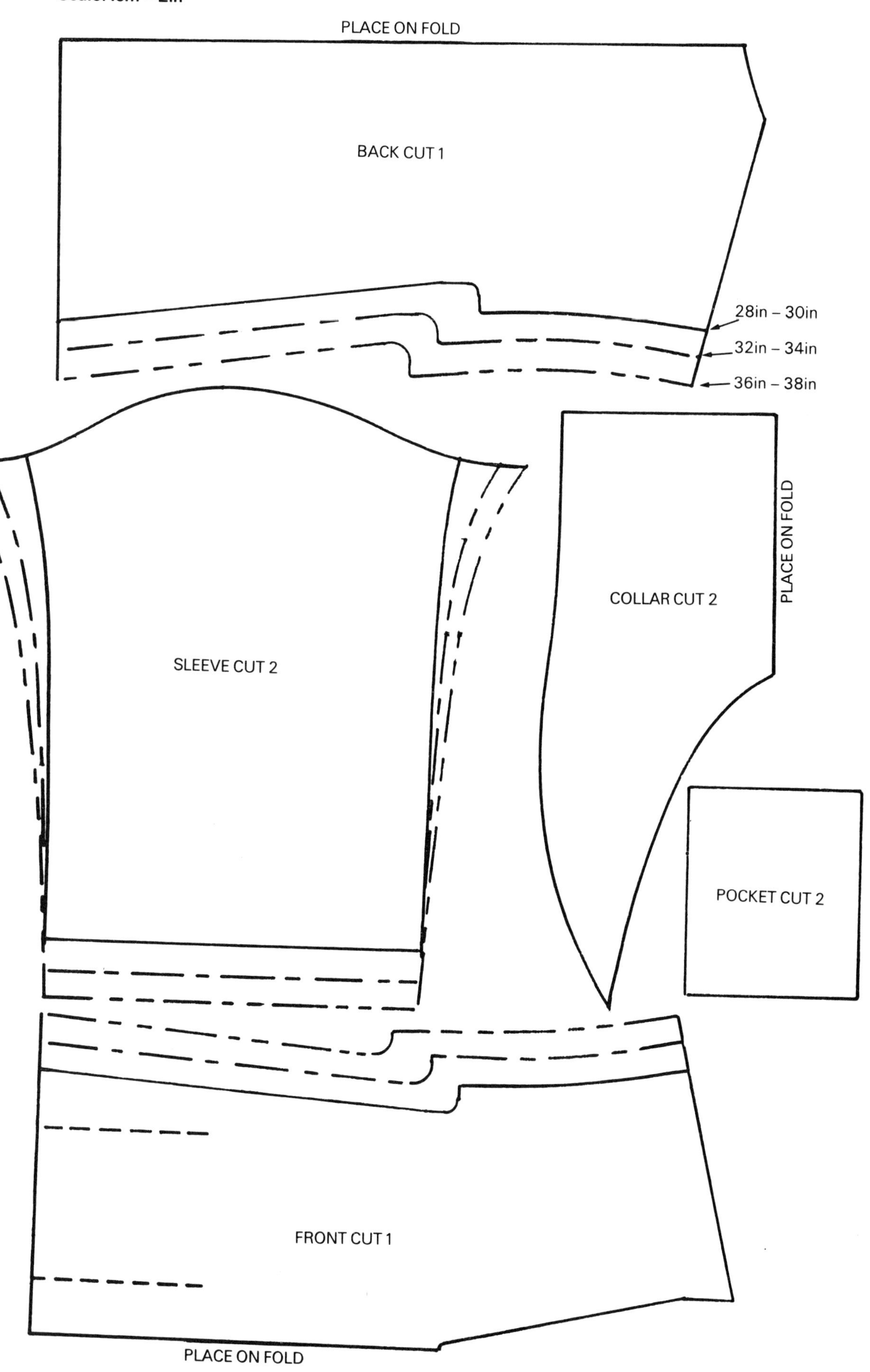

TEGAN'S BOOB TUBE

Scale: 1cm = 1in

FOLD ALONG THIS LINE FOR ELASTIC CHANNEL

FRONT CUT 1

PLACE ON FOLD

FOLD ALONG THIS LINE FOR ELASTIC CHANNEL

34in

36in

38in

BACK CUT 2

ADRIC'S ANORAK

Scale: 1cm = 2in

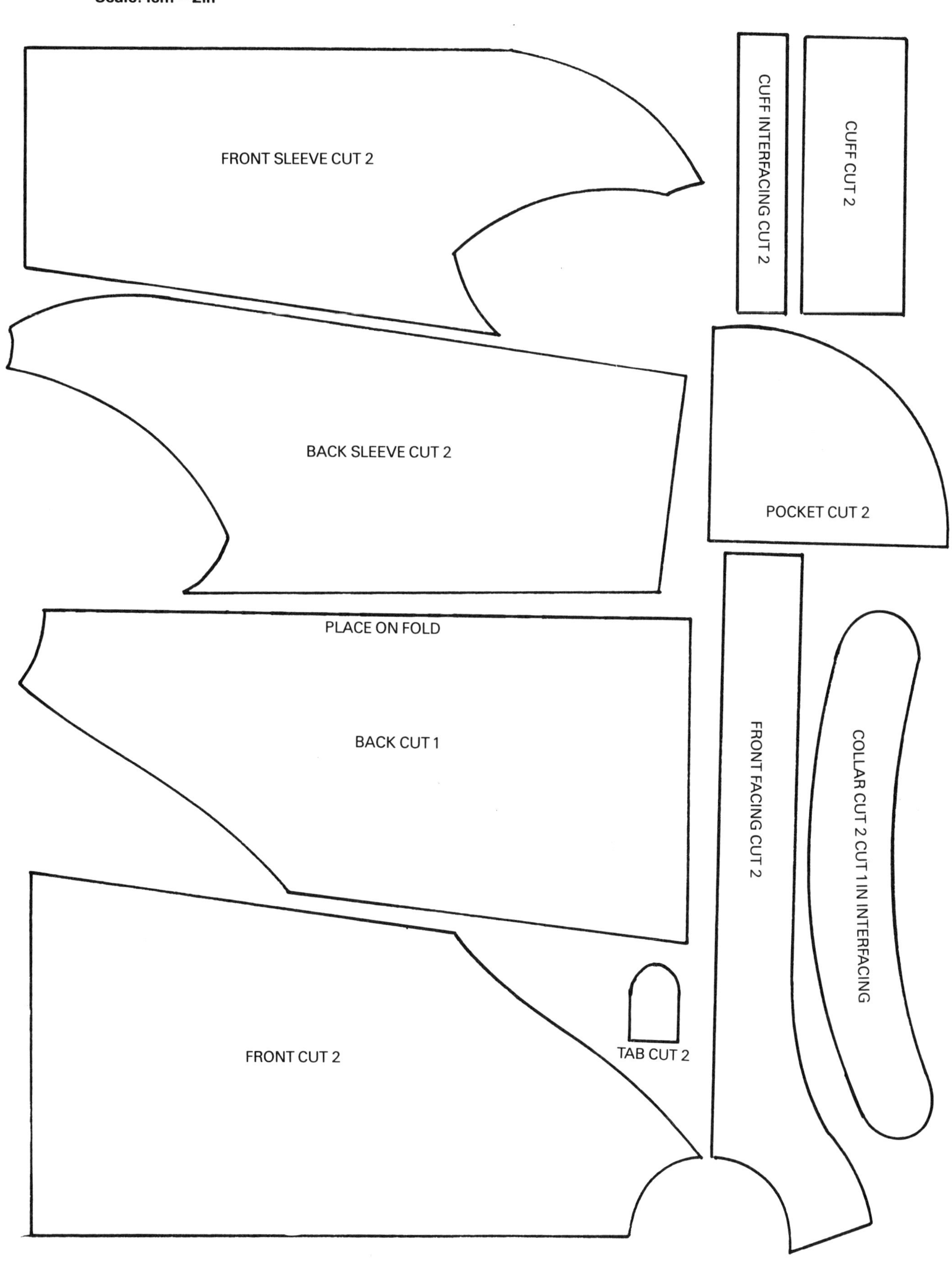

K9 SHOULDER BAG

Scale: 1cm = 1in

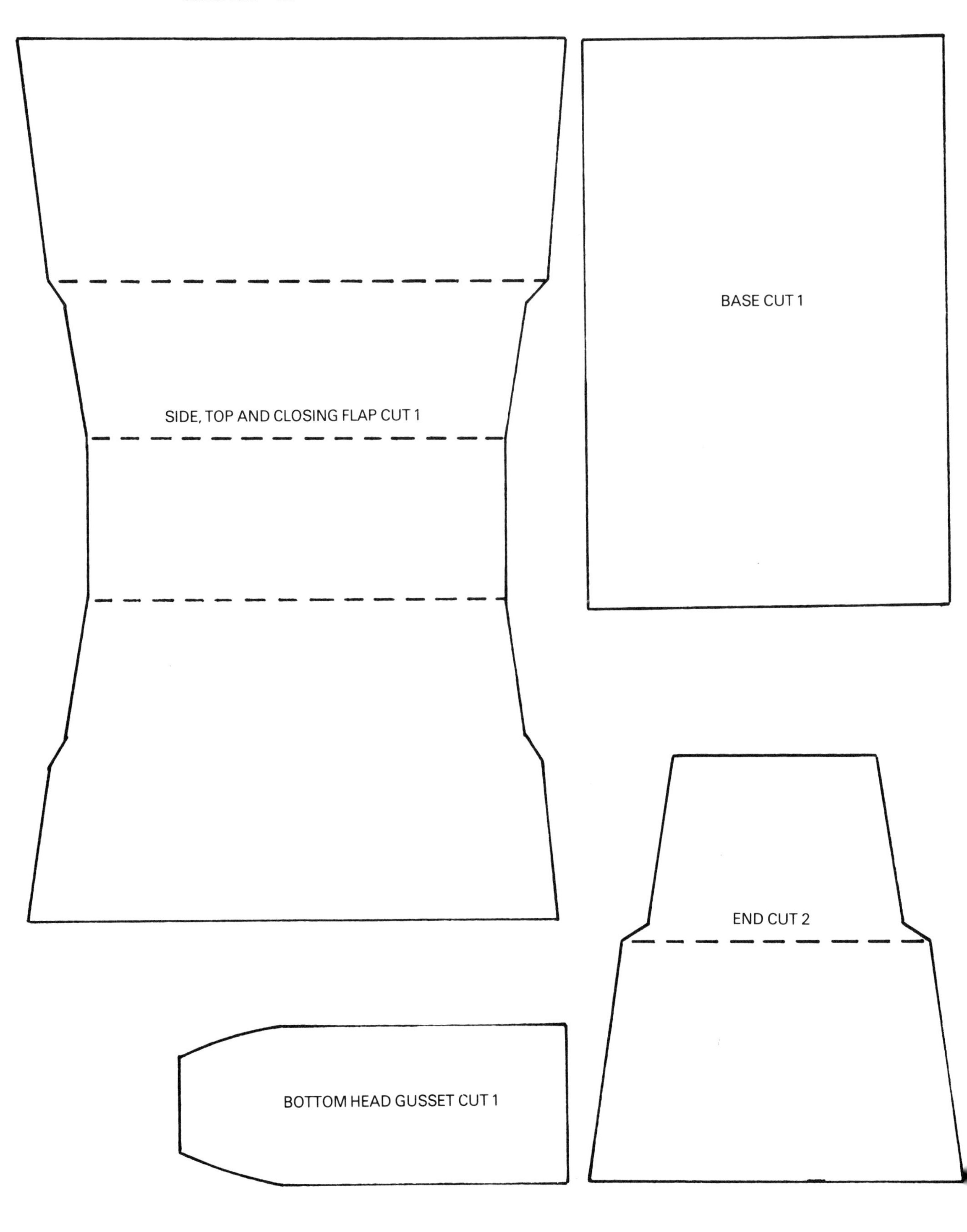

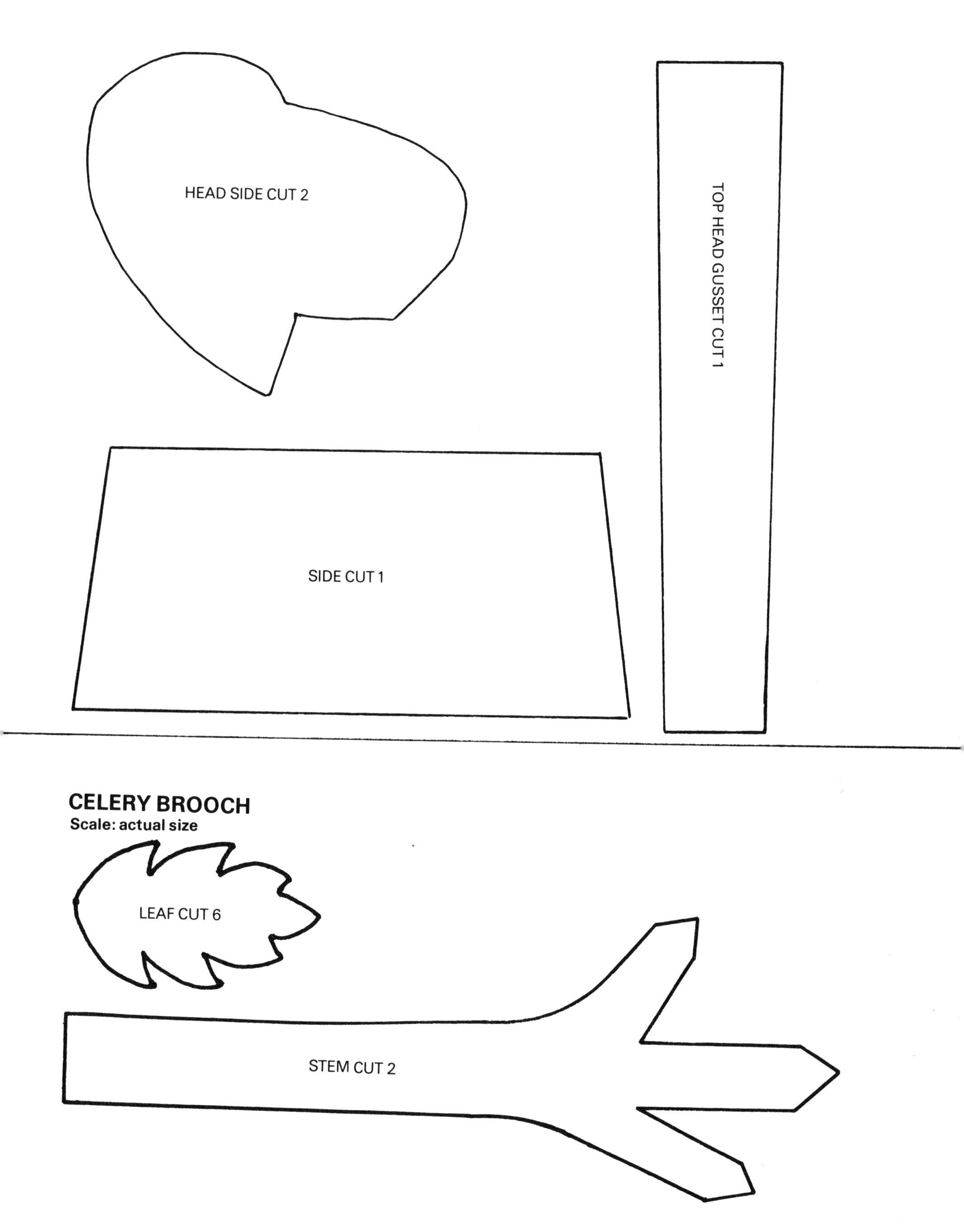
HEAD SIDE CUT 2
TOP HEAD GUSSET CUT 1
SIDE CUT 1
CELERY BROOCH
Scale: actual size
LEAF CUT 6
STEM CUT 2

TARDIS TIDY

Scale: 1cm = 2in

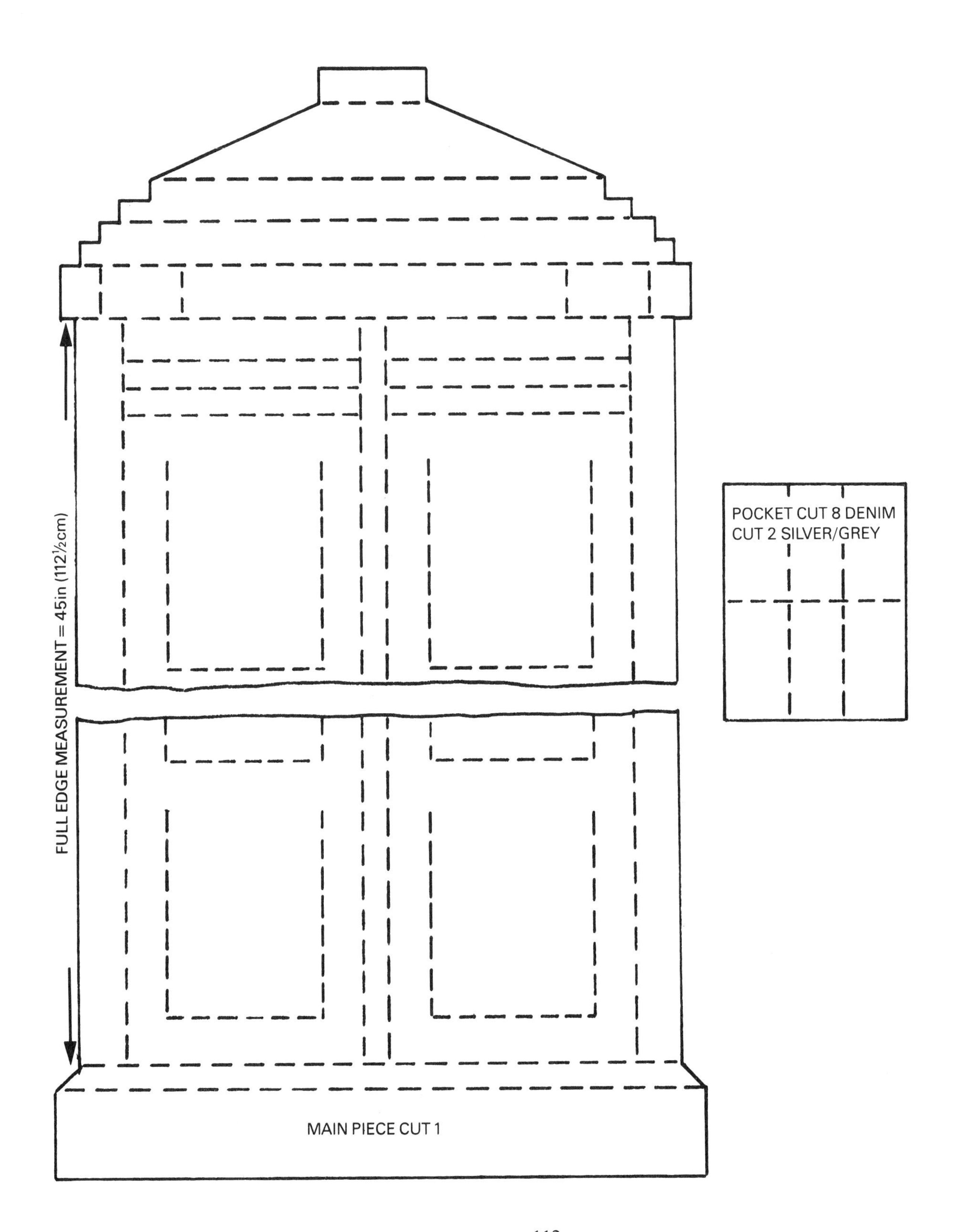

CONSOLE FLOOR CUSHION

Scale: 1cm = 2in

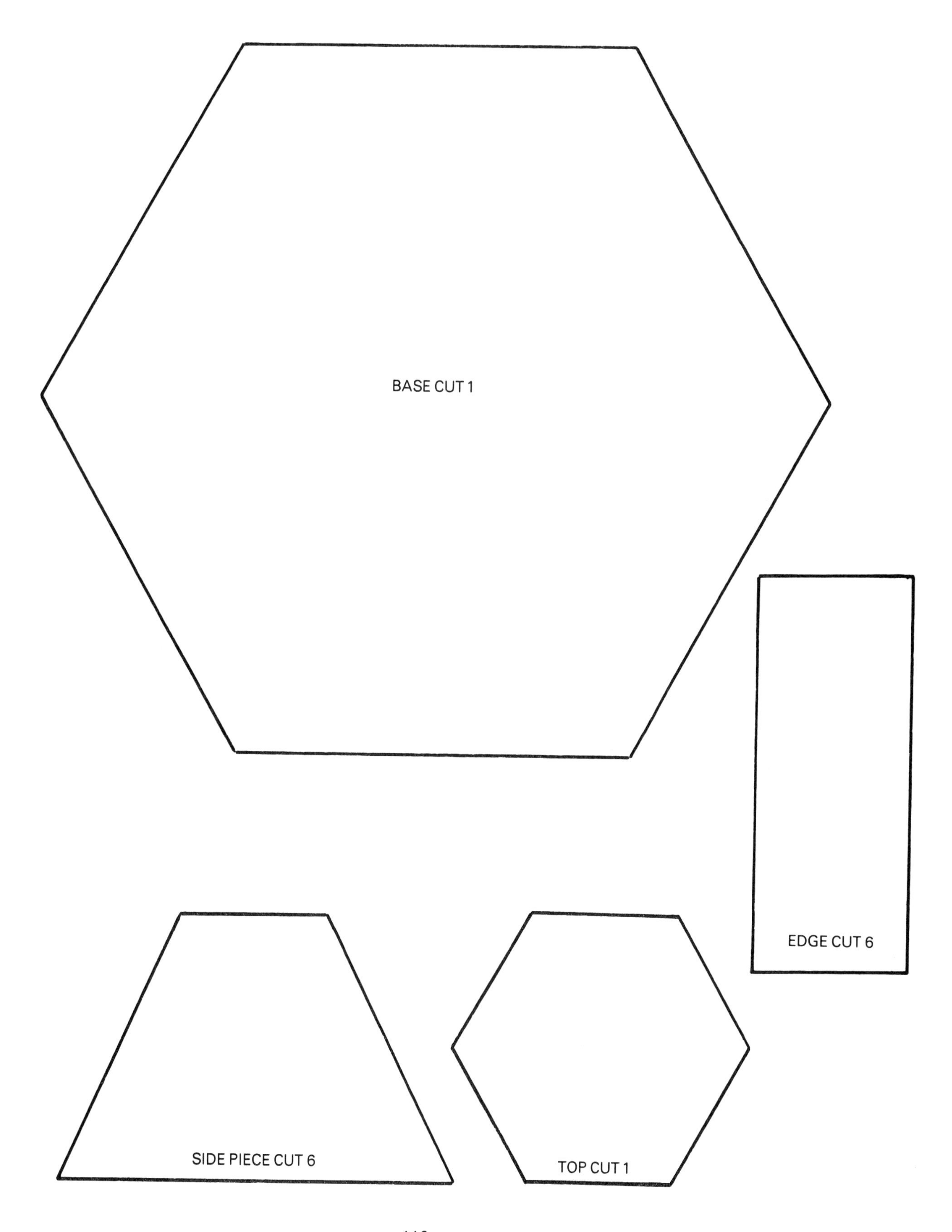

TARDIS CUSHION

Scale: 1cm = 1in

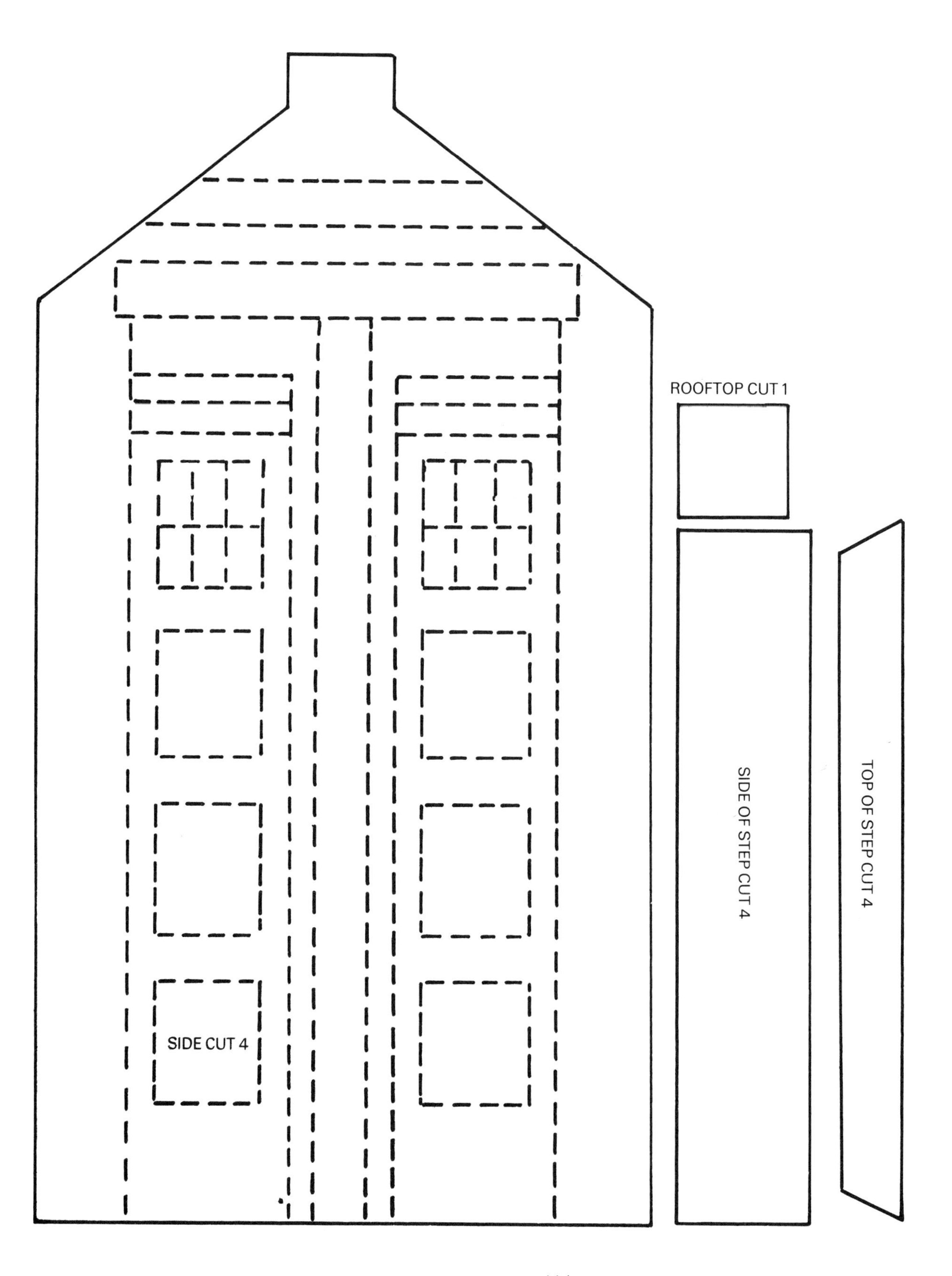

K9 CUSHION

Scale: 1cm = 2in

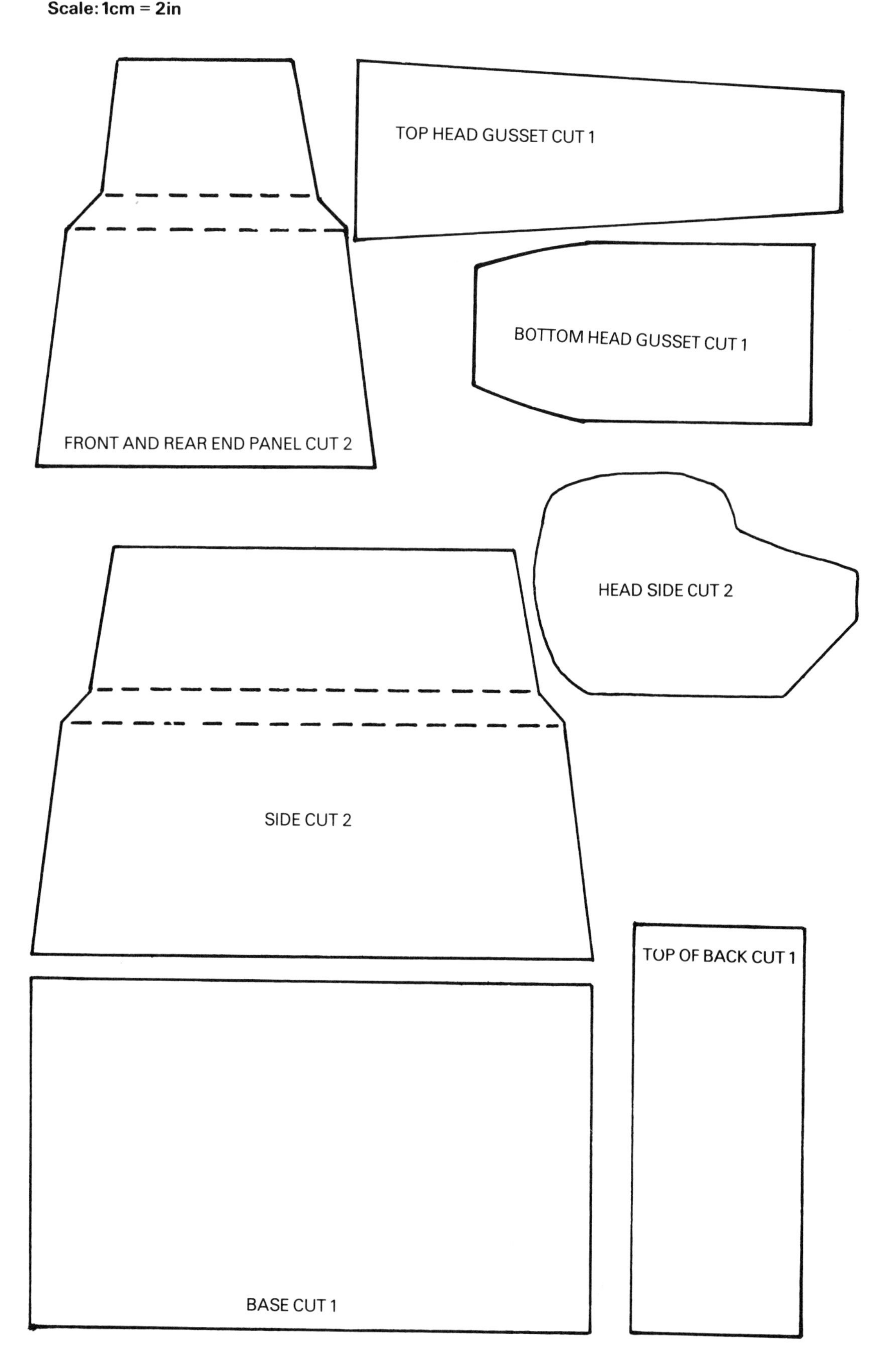

CYBERMATS

Scale: 1cm = 1in

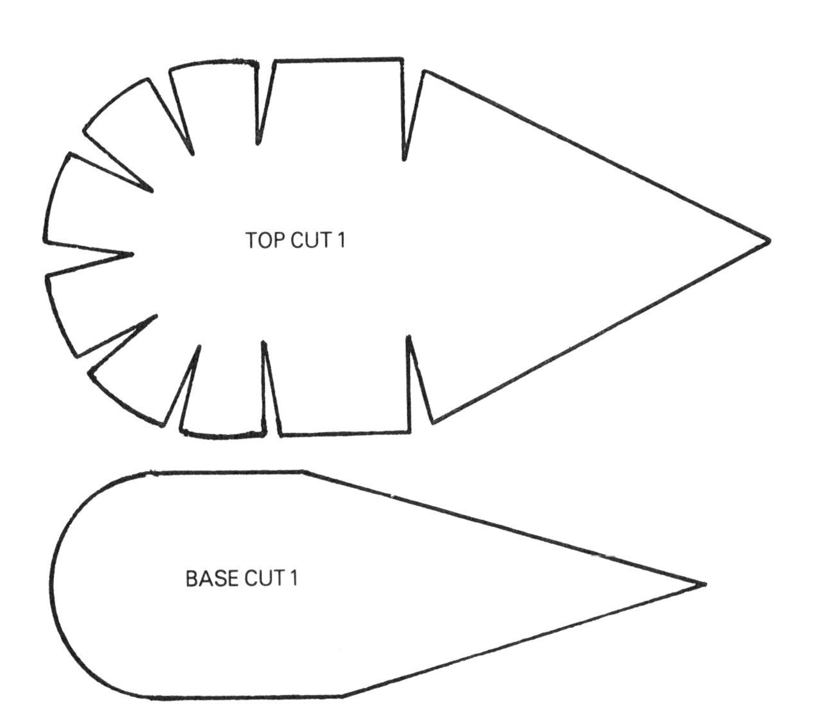

ADRIC'S STAR

Scale: actual size

SEW A NASTY

Scale: 1cm = 1in

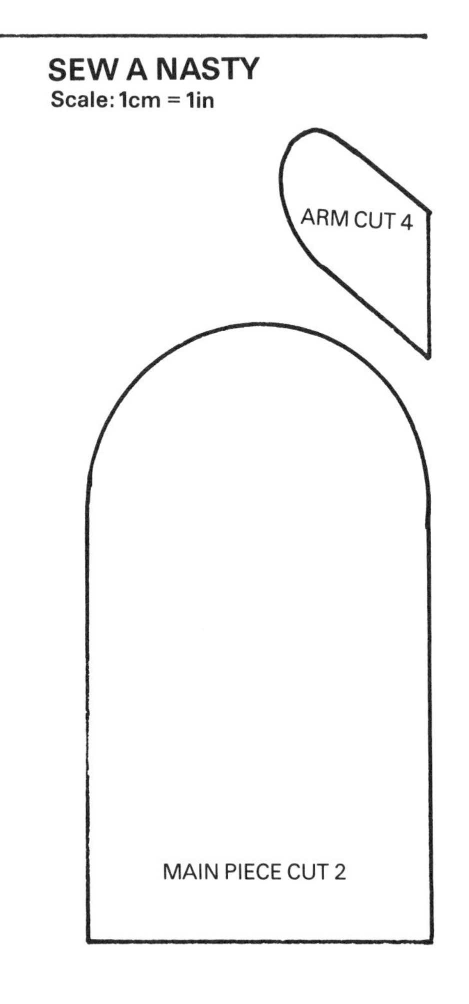

TIME LORDS IN ACTION

Scale: actual size

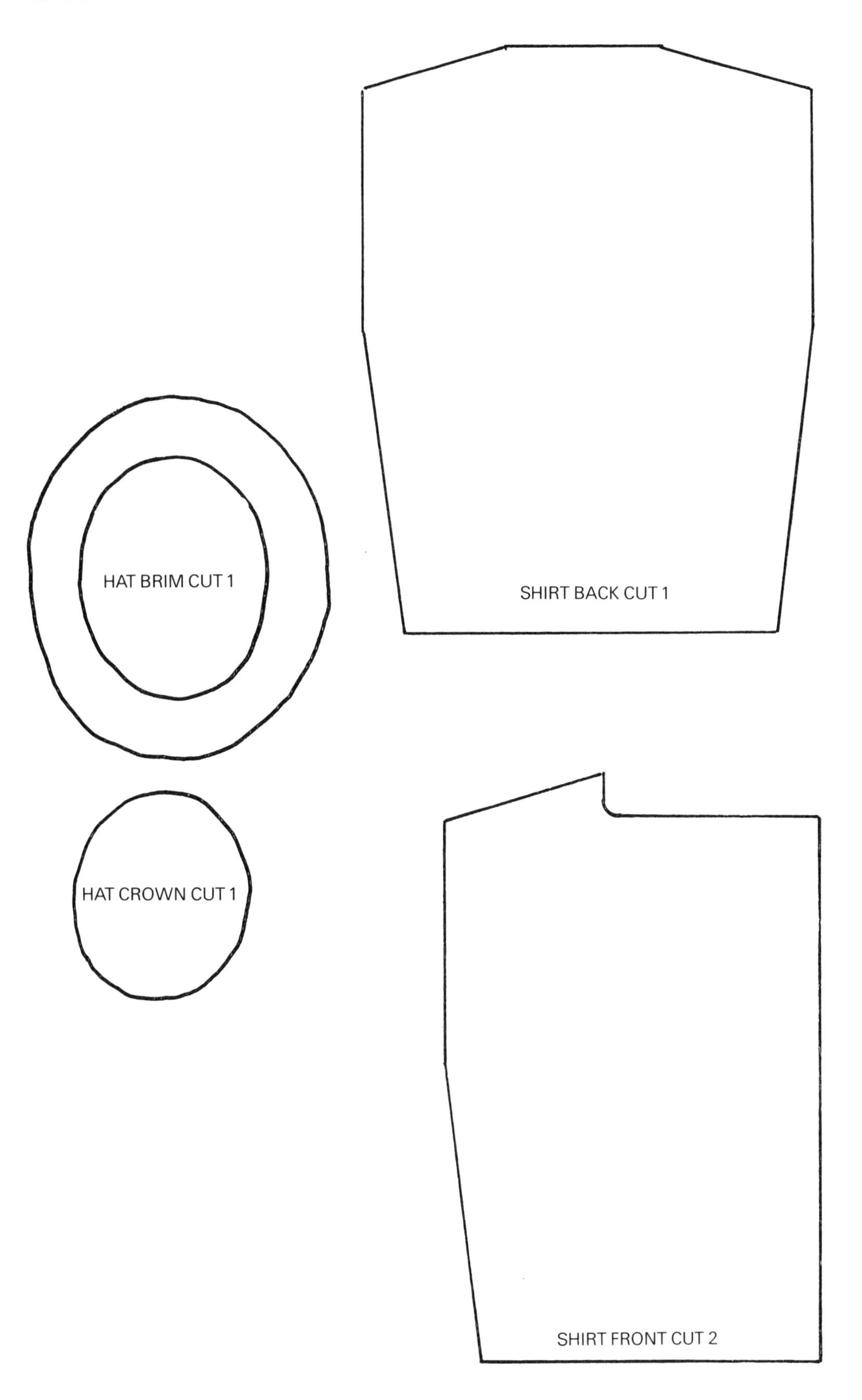

PUPPET THEATRE ☆

Puppets are, and always have been, exciting things on several levels. Traditional puppets have always been a serious art form in many countries – think of the lovely wooden German ones, and the beautiful Indian silhouette puppets. It is possible to become as involved in the fate of the characters in a puppet show, as it is in that of real live actors. There are few people who are unmoved when watching small children roaring with excitement at a Punch and Judy show, or who do not worry about the eventual fate of Pinocchio. At a more simple level, puppets have, for children at home, the charm of doing exactly as they are told, saying whatever words they are given, as well as helping to create stories and plays.

For these plays, it is fun to have a theatre. There are many simple ways of doing this. The puppets can simply appear over the top of the settee, chairs, or a table, while their owner/operators hide below. If you are lucky enough to acquire an enormous cardboard box or carton, the children can be inside it and the puppets can appear over the top. A bit tricky, this, though, if there is a cast of thousands!

More elaborate theatres can be built in wood by capable Dads or Mums in the style of the traditional seaside Punch and Judy booth, but this is very ambitious. A more simple compromise is to use an old-fashioned clothes drier/airer if you have one, the kind than opens out into three sections. Drape the sides, and the bottom of the middle section with towels or sheets and operate the puppets over the top of these.

This theatre (see pages 30–1) has several advantages. It is very easy and cheap to make, but looks spectacular. It can also be made very satisfactorily by the children themselves, with some help with the initial cutting, and because it is still a box, it makes a useful container in which to store the puppets and other props between the shows. If parents want to make the theatre as a surprise present at Christmas, for example, it even makes a super box to hand over all those other presents in!

To make

1. Choose a large sturdy cardboard carton and, if necessary, cut off the flaps, or cut out one side, to give one completely open side, the largest, which then becomes the front. Be careful here, and help younger people with all the cutting, of course.

2. On the back wall of the theatre draw a line parallel with the base and 2in (5cm) above it, ending about 2in (5cm) from the side corners at each end. Draw a similar line on the floor of the theatre, again parallel with the base of the back wall, and 2in (5cm) away from it, ending this line, too, 2in (5cm) from the side

corners at each end. Cut along these lines and also make a cut joining their ends, so removing the corner of the box in a long strip. Youngsters may again need help here, especially if it is necessary to use a sharp knife or a craft knife for the job.

3. Line the box with wrapping paper, wall paper, anything you would like to suggest the sort of scene you want. If you have enough, cover the outside of the box too. Use paper glue, especially the kind in solid stick form, or, even better, double-sided adhesive tape. Cut pieces to shape before you apply any glue, then glue them in place. The theatre here wanted a *Doctor Who* feel, so it is papered in metallic and starry gift wrap, but there are other wonderful gift wraps around now with which you could create a variety of super scenes – jungles and nature scenes, for example. You could of course use any plain paper and draw what you want on it. Be careful with paint, especially water-based paint, as it tends to come off on your clothes.

4. Place the theatre on a table so that the slit overhangs the table edge, and drape the table, preferably to the floor, with a cloth or sheet, or a piece of material, on the front and sides, leaving the back open to accomodate props, spare puppets and for hiding the operators.

5. Make props and additional scenery if you like. Dolls' furniture could be used. For an interior, cut and 'glaze' side windows and doors (rear windows would reveal the operators of course), and make curtains of paper, ribbon or fabric, lace curtains from doilies or snipped tissue paper. The ideas, once you begin are endless. The curtains on this theatre are represented by two pleated strips of wrapping paper stapled (or you could glue or use adhesive tape) one each side of the front opening. It is quite difficult to rig up a system for drawing or raising it when the basic material is cardboard, but if you would like a real curtain you could stick or staple a piece of material all along the top edge of the front, and throw it back over the top when you are ready.

6. To change the scenery in the middle of your play, you could just change all the moveable props, but for a really spectacular scene change why not make two or even more different box theatres and simply change to a new stage for the next scene? Either leave them all ready in a row along the table, curtained so as not to spoil the surprise, or if your table is too small, simply remove one box and replace it with the next. Between plays, you can of course strip out all the decorations inside the theatre and start again.

Let your imagination go, and have fun!

ACKNOWLEDGEMENTS

Many thanks go to the BBC for their help with background information, and also to all of the following: Acorn Computers Ltd of Cambridge, England, who supplied the BBC Micro computer; Bandai Ltd of Guildford, England, who supplied the Ulysses range of space models; JTI Ltd of Tavistock, England, who supplied the Tente range of space model kits; The Pallitoy Company of Leicester, England, who supplied the Action Man range of figures; to Sue Loveridge for the How-to-Knit drawings; to Alan, Anne-Marie, Emily, Jack, Karl and Walter for modelling; and to Jackie Godson and John Wright Photography for the photographs.

CW00544586